"What would happen if we had womani
answered by those who are practicing wo
and critically reflecting on it from an orga
spective. *The Gathering, A Womanist Church: Origins, Sto*
and Litanies is the first book on womanist ecclesiology. Written by Black women co-pastors and partners in ministry of the first womanist church, this book fills a void in constructive ecclesiology. The authors systematically answer theological and ministry questions such as: 'What is a womanist church?' 'Why are womanist churches necessary?' 'Why now?' 'How does one go about creating a womanist church?' and 'What difference does a womanist church make to church and society?' The Gathering is committed to a non-patriarchal, non-misogynist, and non-sexist ecclesiology. The authors demonstrate that it is possible to embody co-equality in all aspects of ecclesial structure, from its co-pastors and partners in ministry to the community in order to empower all people. If you have been wondering if womanist ecclesiology is more than a vague concept, here you will find stories of womanist church as a living reality. The authors share their scholarly knowledge and experiences of womanist church, biblical exegesis, sermons, and litanies to demonstrate that womanist church is a living reality and that the time for womanist churches to multiply is now. This book is a keeper for all who aspire to an ecclesiology that takes seriously Black women's lives, Black women's wisdom, and Black women's church leadership in a world of crucifixion in which embodied, resurrected souls have the last word."

—DR. KAREN BAKER-FLETCHER
Professor of Systematic Theology, Perkins School of Theology,
Southern Methodist University

"Like the first-century women disciples of Jesus in the early Christian house churches, the co-pastors of The Gathering, a womanist community of faith in Dallas, Texas, have revolutionized practical ecclesiology by rejecting the institutional misogyny and sexism of the traditional church. This thought-provoking and inspiring resource details the genesis and development of The Gathering; presents research findings of other womanist-centered, cutting-edge religious organizations; and outlines the practical steps in establishing a womanist-based ministry. The authors demonstrate convincingly that Christian ministries steeped in the experiences of Black women embody the physical manifestation of liberation and womanist theological scholarship. Further, they show that womanist ecclesiology leads to the spiritual healing and transformation of those oppressed and downtrodden by white supremacist, hetero-patriarchal capitalist society. *The Gathering, A Womanist Church* portends the hope and future of Christianity for such troubling and challenging times as these."

—REV. DR. TAMARA E. LEWIS
Assistant Professor, Perkins School of Theology,
Southern Methodist University

"When you try something really hard, and you feel God's windy Spirit at your back, and it works, you want to shout it to the whole world: 'Look what God will do! Alleluia!' The women of The Gathering, with the Spirit's help, have done something really hard, and so beautiful. This book is their *alleluia*, and all of us with ears to hear are blessed by it. Shout it from the mountaintops, sisters!"

—REV. DR. KATIE HAYS
Lead Evangelist, Galileo Church, Fort Worth, Texas, and author of
We Were Spiritual Refugees: A Story to Help You Believe in Church

The Gathering, A Womanist Church

The Gathering, A Womanist Church

Origins, Stories, Sermons, and Litanies

Irie Lynne Session
Kamilah Hall Sharp
and Jann Aldredge-Clanton

Foreword by Frederick D. Haynes, III

Preface by Phillis Isabella Sheppard

WIPF & STOCK · Eugene, Oregon

THE GATHERING, A WOMANIST CHURCH
Origins, Stories, Sermons, and Litanies

Wipf & Stock
An Imprint of Wipf and Stock Publishers
199 W. 8th Ave., Suite 3
Eugene, OR 97401

www.wipfandstock.com

PAPERBACK ISBN: 978-1-7252-7462-4
HARDCOVER ISBN: 978-1-7252-7463-1
EBOOK ISBN: 978-1-7252-7464-8

Manufactured in the U.S.A. 08/19/20

Contents

Foreword

I AM CONVINCED THAT if Jesus of Nazareth showed up in the flesh in most churches, he would be turned off and turned away, unwelcome and unrecognized. Many churches that gather in the name of Jesus would discover that he would reject their praise, disrupt their worship agenda, turn over the offering tables, and demolish the pulpit. Jesus would reject the praise of any church that neglects to do the work of justice and interrupt any worship experience that neglects the needs of the hurting, just as the prophet Amos declared and as Jesus demonstrated in the Gospel narratives. The temple cleansing of those who economically exploited the poor is a preview of what the sable-skinned Savior from the streets would do to the offerings of super-sized churches that major in maintenance of their massive facilities but minor in ministry to the marginalized. In one of the Gospel narratives, Jesus welcomes and heals those who weren't supposed to be in the precincts of the temple after he chases the money changers out of the temple. Jesus would be offended by the theology espoused in the pulpit that is sanctioned by empire, ignores the poor, engages in toxic masculinity, and is informed by a top-down hermeneutic that is in bed with injustice while being more capitalist than Christian.

As Jesus searched for a church, I would gladly tell Jesus about a church that has taken his mission and ministry seriously. I would insist that Jesus go to a church where he would feel at home. I would excitedly invite Jesus to attend The Gathering. The Gathering is a womanist church in Dallas, Texas, doing the hard work of creating a beloved Christian community while they impact and transform the community. Jesus feels at home at The Gathering because he identifies so strongly with their liberating and empowering theology that informs their loving ecclesiology. I could see Jesus inspired by the compassionate and welcoming climate that characterizes

The Gathering. Jesus would appreciate and applaud the egalitarian leadership of bold, brilliant, and dynamic Black women who embody and fight to dismantle hierarchy and work in harmony with Jesus at the center of their word, worship, and work. I could see Jesus being blessed and even shouting during the sermons because they are informed by womanism. The Gathering tells us that "womanism is rooted in Black women's experiences of struggle, resistance to oppression, survival, and community building." Jesus identifies with womanism because of his own struggle as a dark-skinned Palestinian under empire, resistance to oppression, survival, and determination to build the beloved community. Since "womanism works for the wholeness of all people and all creation," Jesus would be graciously embraced at The Gathering.

The Gathering, A Womanist Church: Origins, Stories, Sermons, and Litanies tells the phenomenal and unfolding story of this radical, unorthodox, powerful, compassionate, and loving community. This book is a page-turner that provides an enlightening primer of womanist theology, while testifying to the process of building a womanist church. This book is fire, and the sister authors are fierce. For those who are in ministry, this book will challenge you and inspire you to engage in radical ministry informed by womanism. If you have given up on the church because you've been wounded by the church, this book will offer you healing and hope.

In the old school Black Baptist Church, the pastor, upon concluding the sermon, would extend the invitation for worshipers to join Christ and the church with the words, "The doors of the church are open." Sadly, the doors were only open to certain people who would conform to the ideology of the church that was rooted in sexism. The doors of the church weren't open to women in ministry. The doors of the church were closed to those in the LGBTQ community unless they served in music ministry and were content to be second-class citizens. The doors of the church were open with a caveat.

At The Gathering, the doors of the church are truly open. The doors of The Gathering are open, inviting all to come in and experience a beloved community. The doors of The Gathering are open to the outcast and the overwhelmed, the least of these and the lost, the marginalized and those who live on Main Street. The doors of The Gathering are open to all who recognize that the hope of our sick nation, infected by toxic masculinity, the poison of racism, and the brokenness that comes from oppressive hierarchies, is in the ministry, mission, and message of this compassionate community. The doors of The Gathering are also open, inspiring all to go into the world to create the beloved community. The Gathering gathers and then scatters into the world to fight for justice for all, as they dismantle racism and sexism and transform the world. I am convinced Jesus would love this gathering of grace, and I hear God saying from eternity, "Now this is my beloved Body of Christ in whom I am well pleased." Yes, She is!

Rev. Dr. Frederick Douglass Haynes, III
Senior Pastor, Friendship-West Baptist Church, Dallas, Texas

Preface

Womanist Gathering as Public Theology

When I sat down to begin this preface for *The Gathering, A Womanist Church*, I imagined that I would be reflecting on womanist teaching as a site for womanist church, and womanist church as a site for womanist teaching. I imagined, because I added the course *Spirituality and Social Activism in a Time of Trauma* to the Maymester summer schedule, that I would bring much of our focus to the Nashville tornado recovery and COVID-19.

Instead, the last week of May 2020 we are buckling under the weight of a(nother) police officer killing another unarmed Black man. George Floyd could not breath under police restaint. George Floyd died a horrible, violent death at the hands of a police officer who had eighteen prior complaints filed against him. Derek Chauvin has since been terminated from his position and arrested—but he is alive.

George Floyd died calling out "Mama." George Floyd is dead.

His mother, already on the other side of the river, could only receive him; she could not free him from the knee pressed down on his neck. She could not breathe life into lungs as his breath was chocked off by a knee delivering the messages of hate, racism, and death.

George Floyd was murdered. Minneapolis, Atlanta, Detroit, Oakland, Louisville, and cities all across the U.S. are on fire.

We are witnesses to a smoldering liturgy of rage. We need to, we must, gather.

Womanist Pastoral Approach as Public Theology

Womanist pastoral theologians take note of what is happening in the lives of the most vulnerable Black, brown, poor, and disenfranchised bodies and the world. We begin by asking six important questions. What is happening? To whom? How is it happening? Why is this happening? What ethical demands does this situation announce for the pastoral contexts? How are we to respond?

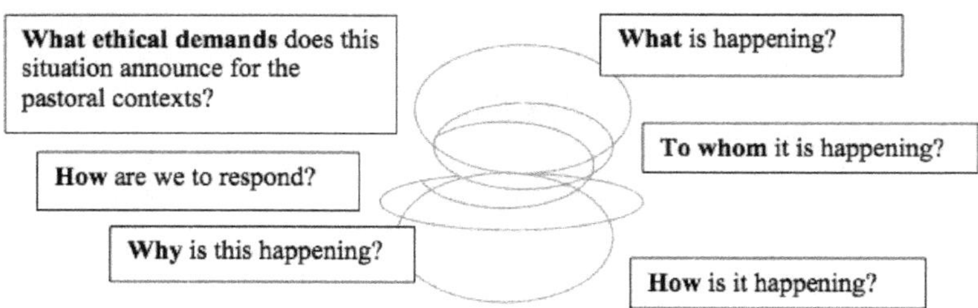

These questions are not asked in linear question and answer process but engage in a recurring cyclical engagement with these pressing questions. In this cyclical or spiral, we deepen the questions by intertwining the realities of social contexts, gender, race, sexuality, gender expression, and education to consider how they are operative forces in communities and individuals' lives. The Combahee River Collective, a Black feminist collective, in their 1978 "Combahee River Collective Statement," raised the need for an analysis of the interlocking nature of Black women's oppression.

> The most general statement of our politics at the present time would be that we are actively committed to struggling against racial, sexual, heterosexual, and class oppression, and see as our particular task the development of integrated analysis and practice based upon the fact that the major systems of oppression are interlocking. The synthesis of these oppressions creates the conditions of our lives.[1]

The Black feminist lawyer Kimberlé Crenshaw referred to these simultaneous and interlocking forces operative in Black women's lives as intersectionality[2]—looking at the convergence of oppressive dynamics rather than focusing on one, race or gender, as the root of suffering and oppression. Womanist pastoral theologians are also sensitive to the ways in which these forces take up residence in Black psyches as internalized negative reflections and representations of blackness. Womanist pastoral

1. "The Combahee River Collective Statement," para. 1.
2. Crenshaw, "Mapping the Margins," 1241.

theologians seek to address these sources of social oppression, psychical malformation, and, as a consequence, spiritual harm, simultaneously.

Womanist Ethnography as Pastoral Listening and Public Theology

Womanist pastoral theology that engages the multilayered experiences of Black life requires practices of listening in and out of the explicitly identified pastoral care contexts. Womanist pastoral and practical theologians increasingly turn to ethnography as a method for conveying "thick" narratives that widen the scope of experience. Just as womanist pastoral care requires capacities of empathic listening, organizing narratives, discernment in community, and sustained theological and spiritual practice, womanist ethnography too requires these capacities. In part because womanist ethnography seeks to make the particularity of Black women's lives the impetus for theological reflection and theological practice. Second, womanist ethnography challenges the assumed hierarchy in models of research that privilege "researcher" over "subject." In womanist ethnography, Black women who agree to share their stories and experiences also demand that womanist ethnographers come to the space not as an interviewer but as a Black woman who has experienced the same or similar encounters with suffering and resistance. The listening space that womanist ethnography demands is one of fluid mutuality, transparency, and care. It is a space that makes ethical demands on all parties—womanist ethnography is not just about acquiring a "good" interview or story. Womanist ethnography has as its stated aim the gathering and telling of Black women's lives because Black women's lives have the capacity to interrogate society, demand justice, celebrate Black life, and make public the relationship between lived experience, justice work, and spiritual and religious practices. Womanist ethnography, then, is not a neutral researcher gathering information from a passive storyteller, but it is a collaboration between a Black woman entering into dialogue with Black women and communities in order to create pastoral, preaching, and ritual practices that embody a public theology grounded in love and the struggle for bringing about a more just world for all people.

Womanist pastoral theology is embodied and expresses a deep theological anthropology that makes the claim that everyone—all people—are created in the image of God. This embodied theological anthropology makes claims about who God is and how God is present and operative in the world. The diversity in all creation is, then, a reflection and expression of the love God has for the world. God is diverse, and this diversity is, or should be, mirrored in communities of faith and in the broader society.

The Gathering, A Womanist Church is a space that embodies its public pastoral theology in song, protest, welcome, worship, and spiritual practices. It takes seriously the need to dismantle the idea that the faith community is to be found solely within the four walls of a building. A womanist public theology stretches itself into the local community and beyond—indeed, into the reaches of cyberspace. The book that Irie Lynne Session, Kamilah Hall Sharp, and Jann Aldredge-Clanton have written is a gift for those who take womanist theology and womanist care seriously. Their commitment to careful theological reflection and a welcoming ecclesiology is evident in their worship and their writing. They have made the vision of womanist church an embodied reality and, therefore, invite others to do the same. I hope others will too.

Rev. Dr. Phillis Isabella Sheppard
Associate Professor of Religion, Psychology, and Culture
Vanderbilt University Divinity School, Nashville, Tennessee

1

Defining a Womanist Church

A WOMANIST CHURCH APPLIES womanism and womanist theology to the creation of a faith community. The Gathering, A Womanist Church in Dallas, Texas, is unique as an embodiment of a womanist church. While other churches may draw from womanist theology, The Gathering uniquely applies womanism and womanist theology to the full life and worship of a church community. The Gathering is the only church founded and identified as a womanist church with "womanist" in the title.

Origins, Definitions, and Significance of Womanism and Womanist Theology

Womanism is rooted in Black women's experiences of struggle, resistance to oppression, survival, and community building. The term "womanist" comes from Alice Walker, literary giant and activist, who is perhaps best known for her book and movie, *The Color Purple*. She said "womanist is to feminist as purple is to lavender." Alice Walker coined the term "womanist" in her 1983 critically-acclaimed work, *In Search of Our Mothers' Gardens: Womanist Prose.*[1]

The creation of this concept was a significant moment for women called to teach religion in academic institutions and to ministry in churches. The term "womanist" is derived from "womanish," a Black folk expression of mothers to female children suggesting being grown and responsible. Therefore, womanist preachers seek to approach the homiletic

1. Walker, *In Search of Our Mothers' Gardens*, xi–xii.

text in a responsible manner, learning more than what's on the surface, and doing the deep exegetical work of looking at the biblical text through a lens of liberation.[2]

For Black women at the crossroads of academic institutions and the Black church, the 1980s was a time of self-definition. While the term "womanist" was introduced to the world in the 1980s, its meaning encompassed the lived experience of generations of Black women in America, who, like their biblical foremothers, were legally, socially, and even spiritually relegated to the edges of church and society. These women by mother wit, sheer will, and passionate determination charted their own course, rewriting definitions of what it means to be Black, female, and made in the image of God. With the Black Southern expression "you acting womanish," mamas, grandmothers, aunties, church mothers, and other mothers confirmed, critiqued, and challenged their girl children to insure that they not only survived, but thrived in a world often configured to destroy their creativity, intelligence, and womanhood.[3]

Definitions of womanism and womanist theology come from a variety of scholars, pastors, and authors. Women and men affirm the transformational significance of womanism.

Dr. Keri Day, currently serving as associate professor of constructive theology and African American religion at Princeton Theological Seminary, asserts that womanism gave her a language, a way of naming her own experience as a Black woman in a "society that does not privilege Black women's knowledge production process, but rather culturally represents Black women as less or substandard or subhuman in a variety of ways."[4]

It was this devaluing of Black women that led to the creation of womanism, according to Rev. Dr. Renita J. Weems, Hebrew Bible scholar and co-pastor of Ray of Hope Community Church in Nashville: "You find yourself in a particular context where there are no Black women's voices, no scholarship by Black women. You find yourself invisible; your voice is not wanted and not heard. The word 'womanist' just caught fire for all of us. It was different from 'feminist.' It was our word. It was what our mothers were calling us, meaning that we were sassy, meaning that we were courageous." She explains that the word "womanist" comes from Black folk Southern

2. "Who Is the Womanist?" *The Gathering*, para. 2.

3. Womanist Institute, "What Manner of Woman."

4. Womanist Institute, "What Manner of Woman."

culture, "meaning you are bold, you break boundaries, and you don't mind doing that in order to accomplish what you have to accomplish."[5]

Rev. Dr. Teresa L. Fry Brown, professor of preaching at Candler School of Theology in Atlanta, Georgia, affirms the significance of Black women's voices: "Black women do have voice, even in institutions that said we didn't, that we were not in history books, that we didn't have a place in church. It was through engagement over a period of time, meeting other women who were in little silos of institutions or in churches that I learned the importance of voice for all people." She celebrates womanists as standing on their principles, articulating "the wit and wisdom of Black women" who came before them, and making way for women who will follow them.[6]

Womanism, that centers Black women's experience, is essential to the wholeness of church and society, proclaims Rev. Dr. Stacey M. Floyd-Thomas, associate professor of ethics and society at Vanderbilt University Divinity School in Nashville, Tennessee. Womanism is not only what the Black church needs but what America needs "if we're truly going to embrace the best of who we are as a people who believe that we are all fearfully and wonderfully made and equally created by God." The mission of womanism is "to make the church whole again and to bring the wisdom that is necessary for us all to be liberated and for none of us to be left behind." She says that if it were not for "Black women, not only in the church, but in society at large, we wouldn't have a keen sense of what freedom is." She describes a womanist: "A womanist is wise. She's radical, but she's traditional. She's self-loving, but she's engaged. She's subjective, but she's communal. She's redemptive, but she's critical."[7]

Dr. James H. Cone, founder of Black liberation theology, celebrates "womanist theology and Black woman" as "essential to the very life blood of what we mean by the Black church, the Black religious experience, the Black community." He commends Black womanist theologians, such as Rev. Dr. Katie Cannon, Rev. Dr. Jacquelyn Grant, and Dr. Delores Williams, for contributing to his "constant development of Black liberation theology."[8]

Pastors also draw from womanist theology in developing sermons about race, gender, and class. Rev. Dr. Jacqueline J. Lewis, pastor of Middle Collegiate Church in New York City, states that she leads "with a womanist sensibility"

5. Womanist Institute, "What Manner of Woman."
6. Womanist Institute, "What Manner of Woman."
7. Womanist Institute, "What Manner of Woman."
8. Womanist Institute, "What Manner of Woman."

in her multiracial, multicultural congregation. "We're always thinking about how to story the gospel by any means necessary." In her congregation "the conversations about race and ethnicity and difference and class take on all kinds of nuances," she says. "I think especially of Alice Walker's definition of 'womanism' as loving all people, understanding that our cousins are pink and beige and chocolate brown like me. That has been so important to me as I think about rehearsing the reign of God here on earth."[9]

Rev. Dr. Frederick D. Haynes, III, senior pastor of Friendship-West Baptist Church in Dallas, tells a story illustrating how womanist theology contributed to changes in his preaching: "I was up preaching, and I made a statement related to Sarah in Scripture. And one of my favorite womanist scholars texted me immediately, 'You don't want to say that. That is offensive. That is oppressive.' The more I took a step back and looked at it, the more it dawned on me that I was a contributor, through that homiletical moment, to oppressing the dominant majority in the congregation. As the senior pastor, I don't want to contribute to that oppression." He gives womanism credit for bringing changes: "Womanism helps us reframe our language. Womanism helps us to be more communal. Black women have so infused and energized the Black church. The Black church needs Black women, but more than that, we need Black women out front leading. We need Black women manifesting all of the gifts that they bring to the table."[10]

Also emphasizing the need for womanist theology and Black women leaders in the church, Rev. Dr. James A. Forbes, pastor emeritus of The Riverside Church in New York City, states: "The viewpoint of Black women is essential for full understanding of what's going on in the world as well as what God's Spirit is trying to stir up among the people. The womanist tradition gave me more of a sense of urgency to lift the Black church out of its sexist orientation." He asserts that "womanist tradition introduces a critical listening to all things; that's actually challenging and strengthening to people who can no longer presume affirmation of everything they say."[11]

Rev. Dr. Mitzi J. Smith, professor of New Testament at Ashland Theological Seminary in Ashland, Ohio, underscores the necessity of womanist biblical hermeneutics: "Womanist biblical interpretation is necessary because it brings a different set of questions that otherwise may not get answered. Questions that need to be addressed in order that we can live together

9. Womanist Institute, "What Manner of Woman."

10. Womanist Institute, "What Manner of Woman."

11. Womanist Institute, "What Manner of Woman."

in a society that respects all voices, that is concerned with the predicament of the least of these among us. We need more and different voices at the table." Often we live by a biblical viewpoint that "causes us to be oppressive toward others" and is "oppressive to us as well, but we have not learned to think about it more critically," she says. "Womanism is an approach that privileges the experiences, voices, traditions, and artifacts primarily of African American women, although there are other women of color who call themselves 'womanists.' In biblical interpretation womanist scholars use a particular perspective, an African American female's perspective, privileging our voices. Our voices are not all the same, but we do have things in common. We privilege our concerns, our voices, our traditions, and read biblical texts from that standpoint, from that hermeneutical framework."[12]

One of the founders of womanist theology, Rev. Dr. Katie Geneva Cannon, charts a "three-pronged systemic analysis of race, sex, and class from the perspective of African American women in the academy of religion." In *Katie's Canon: Womanism and the Soul of the Black Community*, she calls for an inclusive ethic and reveals how Black women have been "moral agents in the African American tradition that combines both the 'real-lived' texture of African American life and the oral-aural cultural tradition vital to African Americans."[13]

Another mother of womanist theology, Dr. Delores S. Williams, emphasizes the distinctiveness of womanist theology. In *Sisters in the Wilderness: The Challenge of Womanist God-Talk*, she explains: "Just as womanist theology has an organic relation to black liberation theology, so does it also have an organic relation to feminist theology." Although "black male liberationists, womanists and feminists connect at vital points," there are "distinct differences" precipitated by the "maladies afflicting community life in America—sexism, racism, and classism." Womanist "god-talk often lives in tension with its two groups of relatives: black male liberationists and feminists."[14]

In *Womanist Midrash: A Reintroduction to the Women of the Torah and the Throne*, Rev. Dr. Wilda C. Gafney also delineates the distinctions between womanism and other liberation movements: "Womanism is often simply defined as black feminism. It is that, and it is much more. It is a richer, deeper liberative paradigm; a social, cultural, and political space

12. Smith, "Womanist Biblical Hermeneutics."

13. Cannon, "A Deeper Shade of Purple," para. 11.

14. Williams, *Sisters in the Wilderness*, 158.

and theological matrix with the experiences and multiple identities of Black women at the center. Womanism shares the radical egalitarianism that characterizes feminism at its basic level, but without its default referent, white women functioning as the exemplar for all women." Womanism is distinct from the "dominant-culture feminism, which is all too often distorted by racism and classism and marginalizes womanism, womanists, and women of color." Womanism "emerged as black women's intellectual and interpretative response to racism and classism in feminism" and "in response to sexism in black liberationist thought."[15]

Rev. Dr. Monica A. Coleman adds to an understanding of the origin and definition of womanist theology as distinct from other liberation theologies. In *Making a Way Out of No Way: A Womanist Theology*, she states: "Womanist theology is a response to sexism in black theology and racism in feminist theology. When early black theologians spoke of 'the black experience,' they only included the experience of black men and boys. They did not address the unique oppression of black women." Feminist theologians "unwittingly spoke only of white women's experience, especially of middle- and upper-class white women. The term 'womanist' allows black women to affirm their identity as black while also owning a connection with feminism." Womanist theology analyzes "religion and society in light of the triple oppression of racism, sexism, and classism that characterizes the experience of many black women." Womanist theologies maintain "an unflinching commitment to reflect on the social, cultural, and religious experiences of black women." Womanist theologies are a "form of liberation theology," aiming for the freedom of oppressed peoples" and adding "the goals of survival, quality of life, and wholeness" for Black women and for all creation.[16]

White women also affirm the need for womanism. Rev. Dr. Serene Jones, president of Union Theological Seminary in New York City, celebrates womanist theologians for giving "life" to her "blood" and making her "excited about being a theologian." She expresses the need for more Black women and womanists at Union: "We need more African American women in the student body. We need more funds supporting women to go into ministry. We need more funds for scholarships. We need a whole faculty full of womanists. That would be glorious!"[17]

15. Gafney, *Womanist Midrash*, 2–6.

16. Coleman, *Making a Way*, 6–11.

17. Womanist Institute, "What Manner of Woman."

Although womanism centers Black women, womanism is not only for Black women. People of all races and genders benefit from womanism and womanist theology. Womanism works for the wholeness of all people and all creation.

Womanism and womanist theology continue to make a significant contribution to theological scholarship and to the lived experience of people. As more scholars and pastors "intentionally do the deeper exegetical work of interrogating the sacred biblical texts to raise up the muted voices of marginalized women, the theological landscape for womanism continues to expand."[18]

The Gathering: Defining and Modeling a Womanist Church

Definitions and analyses of womanism and womanist theology, coming from a wide variety of people, provide a strong foundation for a womanist church. This groundbreaking work finds embodiment in a womanist faith community.

As the only church founded and identified as a womanist church, The Gathering is defining and modeling what it means to be a womanist church. The Gathering puts womanism and womanist theology into practice in a faith community. With an expansive mission, an inclusive welcome, an egalitarian organizational structure, womanist co-pastors and ministry staff, ministry partners, womanist social justice priorities, and valuing of all voices, The Gathering embodies a womanist church.

The mission of The Gathering is "to welcome people into community to follow Jesus, partner in ministry to transform our lives together, and to go create an equitable world." Following Jesus means "responding to the least, last, and lost," and being "intentional" in ministry to the "marginalized, oppressed, and downtrodden." The Gathering examines texts to "do the deeper work of seeing the healing, restorative justice, and liberation in the Scriptures." The Gathering addresses social justice "in a way that raises prophetic voices and issues a rallying cry, speaking truth to power." The Gathering is a community where people of all genders and races work "together to dismantle the systemic structures that seek to oppress people."[19] The Scriptural foundation for The Gathering is Luke 4:18–19: "The Spirit . . . has anointed me to bring good news to the poor

18. "Who Is the Womanist?" *The Gathering*, para. 3.

19. "Who We Are," *The Gathering*, para. 1–8.

. . . to proclaim release to the captives and recovery of sight to the blind, to let the oppressed go free."

The Gathering welcomes all people. The Gathering demonstrates that a womanist church is not just for women and not just for African Americans, but that a womanist church is for all people—all genders and races and cultures and experiences. This inclusive welcome begins each worship service: "Welcome to The Gathering, A Womanist Church, a community whose faith in Jesus compels us to create worship experiences that address social injustice through womanist preaching and action, to cultivate a healing, learning, and growing community for people who are churched, unchurched, dechurched, hurt by church, and even those who are sick of church. Welcome to The Gathering, followers of Jesus who believe our ministry priorities of pursuing racial equity, LGBTQIA+ equality and dismantling patriarchy, misogyny, and sexism (PMS) are both political and biblical. Welcome to The Gathering, a spiritual community where all are welcome. Really."

Through an egalitarian organization structure, The Gathering also defines and models a womanist church. Co-pastors, ministry staff members, and ministry partners share in preaching, creating liturgies, worship leadership, pastoral care, and administration.

The Gathering's co-pastors and staff are womanists, who model a womanist church through their ministries. Their experiences as Black women inform their sermons, music, and other parts of the liturgy. Co-pastors Rev. Dr. Irie Lynne Session and Rev. Kamilah Hall Sharp employ womanist biblical hermeneutics in their preaching and draw from their stories and from the stories of other Black women. In some worship services the co-pastors do what they call "tag-team preaching," both delivering short sermons, emphasizing their equal partnership. Rev. Dr. Irie defines a womanist as a "Black woman who is progressive in her theology, courageous in her social justice advocacy and activism, fierce in her love of self and others, and actively engaged in work that contributes to the survival and wholeness of all people, Black communities in particular." Rev. Kamilah describes a womanist as caring "about people and about community" and looking "for ways to make the world better by using the experiences of Black women as a starting point."[20] Rev. Winner Laws, minister of congregational care and spiritual support, says that as a womanist, she is "committed to sharing narratives of Black women's experiences to empower all people spiritually

20. "Meet the Preachers," *The Gathering*, para. 2–4.

and to be a voice for those on the margins to find their place in the creation story." Faith Manning, minister of music, asserts that womanism "is the liberation of Black women," and that "when we liberate Black women we liberate the world."[21]

Ministry partners join to embody The Gathering as a womanist church. In worship services, ministry partners participate in many ways, such as leading Communion meditations and prayers, singing in a choir, writing and leading litanies, greeting people, making announcements, and assisting with technology for livestreaming the services online. Ministry partners also share in the administrative work of The Gathering, and in planning and implementing ministry projects. Based on the belief that partnership in ministry creates "a sense of belonging, deeper connection, and vibrancy" in a faith community, The Gathering invites people to be ministry partners, instead of "members." Ministry partners use their gifts to help "fulfill the God-given vision" of The Gathering. They use their voices, networks, platforms, and voting voices to partner in addressing the social justice priorities of The Gathering—racial equity, LGBTQIA+ equality, and dismantling PMS (patriarchy, misogyny, and sexism). Ministry partners are consistent in participating in worship celebrations in person and/or online, consistent in financial support of The Gathering, and consistent in sharing their "God-given talents with The Gathering."[22]

The Gathering also models a womanist church through social justice priorities of racial equity, LGBTQIA+ equality, and dismantling PMS (patriarchy, misogyny, and sexism). The Gathering creates "worship experiences that address social justice issues through womanist preaching and action." Other missional priorities of The Gathering are to "be an authentic and compelling faith community for people who feel a disconnect with the institutional church; be a healing, learning, and growing fellowship for persons marginalized in society; dismantle patriarchy one womanist sermon at a time; discover together how the ministry of Christ calls us to welcome all, really."[23]

In addition, The Gathering defines a womanist church through the innovative time in each worship service called "Talk Back to the Text." This womanist practice values all voices. After each sermon, people in the congregation have an opportunity to make a comment or ask a question about

21. "Gathering Staff," *The Gathering*, para. 2–4.

22. "Partner. Gather Online. Support," *The Gathering*, para. 1–5.

23. "Meet the Preachers," *The Gathering*, para. 8–9.

the text and the sermon. The preacher or preachers, if they have preached "tag-team" sermons, will then respond and give opportunity for others to respond. This practice includes not only people attending The Gathering in person, but also those attending online. People in the online congregation can send their comments and questions. This inclusive, egalitarian practice gives everyone an opportunity to participate. A person does not have to be a ministry partner or regular in attendance to make comments and ask questions. "Talk Back to the Text" is open even to first-time visitors. A womanist church includes and values everyone, contributing to the wholeness of all.

Womanism and womanist theology have brought transformation to academic institutions, churches, individuals, and society. A womanist church expands this transformation through the power of community and ritual experience. A womanist church community practices and embodies womanism and womanist theology. Worship services in a womanist church convert our imaginations as well as intellects. Through the power of womanist liturgies, womanist theology takes root in our hearts and souls. Our actions also change as the creative, liberating rituals permeate our whole beings. A womanist church has great power to touch the heart and change the world.

Our world stands in urgent need of the transformation a womanist church brings. Although The Gathering is the only womanist church at this time, we believe the Spirit will use The Gathering to give birth to many more womanist churches. The Gathering moves forward to fulfill our unique call to define, model, and create a womanist church.

2

Creating a Womanist Church

Before Rev. Kamilah Hall Sharp moved to Dallas to pursue a PhD in Hebrew Bible at Brite Divinity School, her Memphis pastor, Rev. Virzola Law, introduced her to Rev. Dr. Irie Lynne Session. Kamilah and Irie became good friends, sharing their passion for social justice and their call to preach.

Need for a Womanist Church

When Kamilah began visiting churches in Dallas, trying to find a good fit for her family, she noticed numerous churches that did not allow women preachers. Whenever someone told her of a new church to visit, she went to their website and looked at their leadership. Often she found all males in pastoral positions and when there was a woman included, she was over religious education or human resources. She could not attend a church where she would not be able to live into the call to preach that God had placed on her life. Also, she did not want her daughter to be in a church that would place limits on how God could work in her life because she is a girl. In the numerous churches Kamilah and her family visited, they very seldom heard any sermons that included social justice issues and that lifted women in the biblical text or in current times. Social justice, including justice and equity for women, was important to them, so they could not join any of these churches.

While they were still in the process of visiting churches, Kamilah's husband, Nakia, said to Irie, "You should go be Moses." He suggested she go plant a new church. Irie was not interested in planting a church and responded, "No, and if I were to ever do anything, we would have to do it together." Kamilah was just beginning her PhD coursework and caring for her daughter who was in kindergarten and transitioning to a new school, so she was not interested in planting a church either. At that time Kamilah had no desire to be a pastor.

More than a year later, Irie had an idea for a Womanist Seven Last Words service on Good Friday.[1] The service would include seven womanist preachers from various denominations, preaching the seven last sayings of Jesus from the cross, seven minutes each. This unprecedented and forward-thinking vision resulted in seven women gathered on Good Friday in Dallas, Texas, to reimagine, through womanist interpretation, Jesus's seven last sayings from the cross. Each of the seven women brought messages of hope, freedom, and healing, not just for the guests, but for themselves. It was a rarity, even in 2017, for seven Black preaching women to be in one place, at one podium, on one preaching assignment.

To their surprise, the service was very well attended, with a diverse crowd, and well received. Those in attendance embraced this style of liberating preaching and inquired when and where they would be able to experience this again. People asked, "Where can I hear more of this preaching?" Irie and Kamilah responded, "You really can't hear womanist preaching Sunday morning in Dallas." After having this question raised several times over a few months when they preached in other places, they began to ask the question: "What would it look like to have a space where people could come and regularly experience womanist preaching?"

Beginning a Womanist Church

At this time, Rev. Yvette Blair-Lavallais, one of the preachers in the Seven Last Words service, was leaving her position at a United Methodist church. Kamilah and Irie, recognizing there is strength in numbers, invited Yvette to join them at Starbucks to begin a conversation about creating a space for womanist preaching. The idea of having three women working together to carry the load was intriguing. In this first conversation, they discussed what

1. The Seven Last Words or Seven Last Sayings of Christ Good Friday Service is a tradition in the Black Church that brings together the community to commemorate the final words of Jesus Christ while nailed to the cross. Seven preachers, typically men, proclaim the seven last sayings spoken by Jesus from the cross.

a space for womanist preaching might look like if they worked together. They asked questions: "Who do we envision in the space? What would the space look like? What would be important to us?" After their first meeting they took time to pray and give thought to each of these questions.

When they came back together, they decided that they wanted to create space for womanist preaching in Dallas. In this conversation, they all lifted three concerns as important: womanist preaching, social justice focus, and affirming LGBTQIA people. They agreed that a space for womanist preaching would be healing, authentic, and necessary. The space would be healing because they knew people who had been hurt by life and the church. The space would be authentic because they knew they would show up authentically and make room for others to be their authentic selves as well. In this space, people would not have to pretend to be someone other than who they were. The space would be welcoming to all people. They knew that no space like this was available to them. The space was necessary because there were many people who were being wounded by harmful interpretations of biblical texts, hurt by church, and disenchanted with Christianity.

They also agreed on three missional priorities: (1) racial equity, (2) LGBTQIA inclusion, and (3) the dismantling of patriarchy, misogyny, and sexism (PMS). Equally important, the space could not have a hierarchical framework. For this reason, each of them would have equal input and an equal vote on everything, and they would call themselves "co-leaders." The space would not be a "church," but a place where people could gather and worship. While this may sound like a church, they were not setting out to start a church, so there was no need for them to be referred to as "pastors."

In order to properly prepare, they agreed to take some time to find a location and make sure all the components were in place to ensure success in creating this new space. Irie and Kamilah are both ordained in the Christian Church (Disciples of Christ), so Irie sent an email to the Disciples of Christ Area Minister, asking him to send a message to local churches to see if anyone would agree to offer them permanent nesting space. They were creating this space with no support from any denomination and few personal resources; hence, they did not want to incur a large overhead expense that would take away from their ability to minister effectively. There were five responses from different churches on the day the email was sent. Kamilah, Irie, and Yvette lived south of Dallas, and the churches that initially offered them space were farther north. A few days later, Rev. Ken Crawford, the new pastor of Central Christian Church (Disciples of Christ), also responded, offering them space. Irie was a member of this church, Kamilah had attended several times, and they both had preached at Central. This was the location they were hoping to get because it was more centrally located and a wonderful facility.

Now with a secure location they began to plan an inaugural service. Yvette, Irie, and Kamilah decided to have a one-hour service on Saturday. For them it made sense to have a Saturday service because there were many people who were interested in participating who worked in various churches on Sunday. Also, there are thousands of churches in the Dallas-Fort Worth area, but few offer services on Saturday. They then considered what the service would look like, and they agreed to have "Greet & Tweet," weekly Communion, rotating and tag-team womanist preaching, and a question and discussion time called "Talk Back to the Text."

For weeks they advertised on social media outlets. On Friday evening before the inaugural service, they set up Central Christian Church's fellowship hall. Since they knew they were creating space for people who were hurt by church, they thought people would feel more comfortable in the fellowship hall than the sanctuary. The chairs were set up in a half circle with an aisle and the podium was on the floor with the chairs, instead of up on the stage, to prevent a hierarchical visual.

On October 16, 2017, the day of the service, they arrived and began to wait, not knowing if anyone would come. Cars started pulling up on the parking lot, and people began to come into the fellowship hall. Approximately eighty-five women, men, and children of different races attended that first service. Rev. Kamilah, Rev. Irie, and Rev. Yvette tag-team preached, and the service was complete in one hour. It was well received, so they agreed to keep going. The following week they prepared and showed up, wondering if people would come again or if it had been a one-time event. Once again people showed up. It became an ongoing joke among the co-leaders, "Is this the week no one will show up?" Nevertheless, week after week people kept coming and have continued to come every week since they started.

Central Christian Church is a community church that opens its doors to a variety of groups, organizations, and more. Central had booked the fellowship hall for a group's Christmas fundraiser before Irie, Kamilah, and Yvette began holding services there. This meant that in order to have a worship service one week in December of 2017, they would need to move into the sanctuary. Kamilah was concerned about people she thought did not want to be in a church. Reluctantly, they moved the service to the sanctuary and put a podium on the floor so they could be with the people. To their surprise, people loved the sanctuary. A teenage boy who had been attending regularly asked Irie if services could be there from then on. Several others also commented about how they liked being in the sanctuary better. At that time, they realized "The Gathering" was becoming a church. Shortly thereafter, Irie suggested adding "A Womanist Church" to the name; they became "The Gathering, A Womanist Church," and the three of them became co-pastors.

Challenges and Rewards of Creating a Womanist Church

Active on social media, each of The Gathering's co-pastors knew they had to use social media to promote and reach more people. Irie used "Facebook Live" often in her own work, and they agreed to use it for The Gathering. They were concerned that if they streamed the entire service, people in Dallas would not come because they could watch online. The original compromise was to stream only part of the service. After a few weeks, they realized that many more people were watching from outside the Dallas-Fort Worth area and wanted to experience more of the service. So they began streaming the service until the sermon was completed and ended before Talk Back to the Text. At this point they thought the conversations during Talk Back to the Text were intimate, and they did not want to share them online. They began to have more ministry partners online who were consistently watching and indicating they would like to participate in the Talk Back to the Text portion of the worship. During this time they were also noticing that the number of online viewers was steadily increasing to hundreds every week. It became clear that they needed to engage this online community and to keep connected to them as well, so they decided to stream the entire service.

Everything that occurred up to this point happened with only the personal resources of the co-pastors and the support of those who were partnering with them at The Gathering. They agreed not to have members, but ministry partners. Ministry partners are those who attend regularly, either in person or online, support the ministry financially, and use their gifts in the community. Not having enough financial support limited their ability to do some things that they wanted to do. Finances continue to be a challenge to this day.

However, the rewards of creating a womanist church are many. It is rewarding to hear people talk about what The Gathering means to them. People who have not attended church in over twenty years come faithfully to The Gathering. When the co-pastors travel around the country, they meet people who say they feel inspired as they watch The Gathering online week after week. It is a great feeling for the co-pastors to know their ministry is making an impact. Another reward comes from making space for other womanist preachers to be heard. When The Gathering began, the co-pastors stated they would open the pulpit at least once a quarter to allow other womanist preachers a space to preach. The reality is there are many great womanist preachers who do not have the opportunity to preach often because there are not many pastors who afford them an opportunity. These are voices people desperately need to hear. For the co-pastors, knowing God has used them to create space for other womanist preachers to be heard is beyond wonderful. Each woman who preaches at The Gathering is paid an honorarium because the co-pastors know all too well how women are not paid equally to men, or sometimes at all, to preach. In creating The Gathering they wanted to make sure they not only preach about justice, but act in just ways.

Toward a Womanist Ecclesiology

The co-pastors of The Gathering, a new model of ministry and church plant, were committed to taking their "spiritual lives into their own hands, refusing to seek permission"[2] to create a womanist ecclesial community that resists white supremacist capitalist patriarchy. They sought to implement a womanist ecclesiology as a strategy of resistance to oppression in both church and society. A womanist ecclesiology as resistance is a direct result of Black clergywomen's experiences in the North American Church with the quadripartite oppressive realities of racism, sexism, classism, and heterosexism. These injustices are forcing them to "forge new pathways to escape religious oppression, marginalization, and colonization while remaining connected to Spirit."[3]

The North American Church has been derelict in its Jesus-identified mission of liberating the oppressed. Even so, Black clergywomen, including scholars and theologians, are forming ecclesial communities outside

2. Watson, *Introducing Feminist Ecclesiology*, 55.

3. Coleman, *Ain't I A Womanist Too?*, 79.

institutional and denominational structures to find healing, wholeness, social justice activism, and the freedom to use and maximize their God-given gifts to transform church and society. Research bears out that, "for a large number of women, the patriarchal and institutional church is no longer a meaningful framework. They begin to create new forms of being church often in small informal gatherings of women (sometimes men) who celebrate liturgies, read Scripture and work for social justice."[4]

When Rev. Irie, Rev. Kamilah, and Rev. Yvette started dreaming and visioning of The Gathering, they didn't have in mind a church. In fact, because of the baggage they carried from previous experiences with church (abuse, sexual assault, and racial trauma), they chose not to call their gathering a "church." At first, they were simply "The Gathering." However, people who began to journey with them helped shape and name the community "church." Rev. Dr. Irie, one of the co-pastors of this new model of church, initially led by a partnership of three Black seminary-trained clergywomen, realized she was in a perfect position to study womanist ecclesiology. She wanted to understand more in order for their ecclesial community not only to survive, but also to thrive.

Eager to learn more about creating a vibrant, thriving womanist ecclesial community that would have longevity, Irie applied for a Pastoral Study Project grant from the Louisville Institute.[5] In 2019 she received a $15,000 grant to work on a research project titled "Womanist Ecclesiologies: Black Clergywomen Resisting White Supremacist Capitalist Patriarchy." Then she embarked on a journey of discovery—a fact-finding mission. She set out to explore and find answers to questions that have arisen out of her ministry with The Gathering, A Womanist Church: (1) What is a womanist ecclesiology? (2) How can a womanist ecclesiology empower Black clergywomen to partner in shaping communities that resist white supremacist capitalist patriarchy and liberate the oppressed? (3) What denominational and/or funding support is needed for womanist ecclesial communities to thrive? She studied five Black clergywomen-led ministries: Middle Collegiate Church in New York City; Lewa Farabale, A Womanist Gathering in St. Louis, Missouri; Pink Robe Chronicles, in Winston-Salem, North Carolina;

4. Watson, *Introducing Feminist Ecclesiology*, 54.

5. In late 1990, Lilly Endowment Inc. (an Indianapolis-based private philanthropic foundation) launched the Louisville Institute, based at the Louisville Presbyterian Theological Seminary. The Pastoral Study Project (PSP) awards pastoral leaders up to $15,000 to pursue a pressing question related to Christian life, faith, and ministry.

City of Refuge in Los Angeles, California, and Rize Community Church in Atlanta, Georgia.

To gain clarity for her research, Irie developed working definitions for key terms: "ecclesiology," "womanist ecclesiology," and "white supremacist capitalist patriarchy."

She defines "ecclesiology" as "the theological interpretation of what it means to be church," highlighting the work of Natalie K. Watson in *Introducing Feminist Ecclesiology*. Because the theological meaning of church has been subject to patriarchal interpretations, Watson argues for an ecclesiology over against a discussion of women *in* the church or women *and* the church. She maintains, women *are* church.[6]

Until she began her research, Irie had never read a book or article that referenced "womanist ecclesiology." She discovered a YouTube video featuring Bishop Yvette Flunder, preaching a sermon titled "A Womanist Ecclesiology."[7] While Bishop Flunder doesn't provide a formal definition of a womanist ecclesiology, she does describe its manifestation. Flunder envisions a womanist ecclesiology in response to what she calls, "unbridled patriarchy."[8] She explains: "There needs to be an ecclesiology or a way in which we see God and ecclesia—the community of the faithful, from a womanist perspective. That means, home and heart are important; it means all our children matter; it means health is everyone's right; it means there is no group of people upon whom everyone else can step up from at that group of people's expense."[9] Mining Bishop Flunder's sermon "A Womanist Ecclesiology" for wisdom, Irie defines a womanist ecclesiology as "ways of thinking theologically about doing and being church that take into account the norms, practices, ethics, wisdom, survival strategies, and lived experiences of Black women which lead to the liberation and thriving of all people."

The work of bell hooks informs the definition and application of the phrase "white supremacist capitalist patriarchy" to capture all the ways in which Black women experience the intersections of oppression. In "bell hooks: Cultural Criticism & Transformation," we gain clarity for her rationale in using the phrase:

6. Watson, *Introducing Feminist Ecclesiology*, 1.
7. Flunder, "A Womanist Ecclesiology."
8. Flunder, "A Womanist Ecclesiology."
9. Flunder, "A Womanist Ecclesiology."

> I began to use the phrase in my work "white supremacist capitalist patriarchy" because I wanted to have some language that would actually remind us continually of the interlocking systems of domination that define our reality and not to just have one thing be like, you know, gender is the important issue, race is the important issue, but for me the use of that particular jargonistic phrase was a way, a sort of short cut way of saying all of these things actually are functioning simultaneously at all times in our lives and that if I really want to understand what's happening to me, right now at this moment in my life, as a black female of a certain age group, I won't be able to understand it if I'm only looking through the lens of race. I won't be able to understand it if I'm only looking through the lens of gender. I won't be able to understand it if I'm only looking at how white people see me.[10]

White supremacist capitalist patriarchy speaks to the ways in which Black women, on a daily basis, experience life. All aspects of Black women's lives, even those parts that are positive and nurturing, are negotiated with resistance through the prism of white supremacist capitalistic patriarchy—the interlocking systems of race, gender, class, and age discrimination.

In her research, Irie found no academic or scholarly resources specifically addressing a theological constructive framework for a womanist ecclesiology. While there are, in fact, numerous books and articles on Black women in the Black Church, none highlight the formation of church vis-à-vis a womanist theoretical lens.

Although there is indeed a dearth of academic material relative to a womanist ecclesiology, she discovered scores of Black clergywomen currently engaged in what Lyn Norris Hayes coins as "practical womanism"[11] or what Irie refers to as "practical womanist ecclesiology."[12] She found myriad ways and platforms in and through which Black clergywomen are engaged in practical womanist ecclesiology. In other words, there are Black clergywomen living out a womanist ecclesiology in their respective congregations, digi-church ministries, Cyber Assemblies,[13] and womanist gatherings

10. hooks, "bell hooks: Cultural Criticism," para. 16.

11. Hayes, *Digging Deeper Wells.*

12. Irie Session first heard the term "practical womanism" from Lyn Norris Hayes when Lyn contacted Irie about using *Murdered Souls, Resurrected Lives* as a source in her dissertation. The term adds nuance to this work on developing a womanist ecclesiology. In early April 2020, Irie contacted Lyn for permission to use the term in this work. Lyn said she was honored to give permission.

13. Sampson, "Going Live," para. 1.

even though they do not identify their community as "church," or *ekklesia*. Building upon Hayes's definition and articulation of "practical womanism," Irie defines "practical womanist ecclesiology" as the "performance of a womanist hermeneutic in the everyday lived experiences of Black women in order to resist oppression in its myriad manifestations and facilitate communal flourishing and wholeness." A womanist hermeneutic is embodied and articulated in the thinking, being, and doing of Black women. Because womanists learn to work around systems of white supremacist capitalist patriarchy, a practical womanist ecclesiology of necessity is wide and broad enough not to be confined to a building that requires maintenance or a mortgage. As God's Spirit "blows wherever it wishes" (John 3:8 CEB), so are the creative contours of a practical womanist ecclesiology.

Irie's research project revealed in very practical ways that, like God's Spirit, the articulation and implementation of a practical womanist ecclesiology cannot be contained, confined, or controlled by denominational, judicatory, or economic systems, or by institutional structures or ideological frameworks that undermine its premise. Her interviews with womanist clergywomen clarified this reality. For example, the co-conveners of Lewa Farabale: A Womanist Gathering in St. Louis realized they had "to do something different." Rev. Lorren Buck, one of the founders of Lewa, remembered sharing with her colleagues: "We can't continue to repeat what has been placed before us and think that is going to be sufficient in liberating women, specifically, not Black women. Because the church is full of Black women who don't have the equal voice and say of their male leadership that believes that their role is really to support the vision of a man with their labor and with their money . . . everything. And that Black women should gladly do it without question." The three Black clergywomen who founded Lewa had an epiphany born of the Spirit: "What if there was a church that had three pastors, one that resisted hierarchical arrangements?" They had no location, limited financial resources, and no denominational support. What they did possess was a prophetic knowing, that is, an organic way of knowing the deepest needs of a certain segment of society and strategies to meet those needs. In her book *Toward a Womanist Ethic of Incarnation: Black Bodies, the Black Church, and the Council of Chalcedon*, womanist ethicist Eboni Marshall Turman describes this prophetic knowing as a womanist epistemology. A womanist epistemology emerges from a posture of radical subjectivity that "resists notions of black women as passive subjects and rather determines that their distinctive consciousness empowers them to proactively engage and shape their own vindication." Turman argues that Black women are not "broken subjects." On the contrary, "radical subjectivity allows for a revaluation of the white racist, patriarchal, capitalist system of values that subjugate black women by privileging black women's embodied experiences rather than oppressive ideologies, theologies, and practices."[14]

A Constructive Framework

From onsite interviews and participant observations, Irie discovered a constructive framework for a womanist ecclesiology, consisting of at least six components. A womanist ecclesiology is *artistically expressive, social justice-oriented,* informed by a *communal Christology, organically trauma-informed,* maintains *God is Universal,* and situates *womanist preachers as primary proclaimers.*

1. Artistically Expressive

   The ministries of the clergywomen Irie observed are artistically expressive. Each displayed creativity of color, vibrant visual imagery in clothing and symbols, stirring music, and creative use of digital spaces and social media apps. For example, as we were in the process of writing this book, the world was hit with a pandemic, COVID-19, the likes of which we had never seen before. Among other adjustments required to ensure the safety and well-being of each person, religious leaders were forced to reimagine processes for carrying out worship and other religious gatherings. What became clear was that there was a group of people, Black clergywomen, already navigating efficiently and creatively alternative modes of communicating spiritual and religious services and conversations. In an article titled "While More Black Churches Come Online Due to Coronavirus, Black Women Faith Leaders Have Always Been Here," Candice Benbow, theologian, essayist, and creative, describes the prophetic innovation of Black clergywomen as a response to white supremacist capitalist patriarchy and heteronormativity: "While some congregations have always had a digital presence, there is one group that has been most consistent with providing ministry in the digital realm. Using social media apps,

14. Turman, *Toward A Womanist Ethic*, 157.

streaming platforms and websites, Black women have created their own spaces to do the work of faith and spirituality."[15]

Black clergywomen, such as Rev. Dr. Melva Sampson, curator of Pink Robe Chronicles, and Ree Belle and Rev. Lorren Buck of Lewa Farabale, as a strategy of resistance, had already carved out digital spaces for themselves to preach, teach, write, and facilitate social justice organizing in order to "do the work their souls must have."[16] These resistance strategies included art, rituals, and curating spiritually expansive space—grounded in sound theological reflection. As a means of survival and subsequent thriving, Black clergywomen were ahead of the curve in taking ministry online by crafting their own digital resumes. The North American Church can benefit from Black women as connoisseurs of creativity by consulting and contracting with them to develop relevant digital ministry that is also artistically expressive, thus speaking to the soul.

2. Social Justice Orientation

Irie's exploration of the ministries of six clergywomen made apparent the social justice orientation of a womanist ecclesiology. Each clergywoman is engaged in *ministry in the street*. "Ministry in the street" as described by Rev. Dr. Maisha Handy, senior pastor of Rize Community Church in Atlanta, is "resistance to empire." Bishop Yvette Flunder, senior pastor of City of Refuge in Los Angeles, describes their social justice ministry this way: "It means all our children matter; it means health is everyone's right; it means there is no group of people upon whom everyone else can step up from at that group of people's expense." Because Bishop Flunder sees "a connection between hatred and abhorrence of LGBTQ persons and an idea that cheapens the value of women and girls," City of Refuge has a robust LGBTQIA+ ministry. Rev. Dr. Jacqui Lewis, senior pastor of Middle Collegiate Church in New York City, explains that their first social justice issue was feeding folks with HIV/Aids, which then led to addressing economic injustice, then a living wage and paid time off. Dr. Jacqui and Middle Church operate with a global understanding that we're all connected. She says, "If someone else is hungry, our stomachs are

15. Benbow, "While More Black Churches Come Online," para. 3.

16. This is a saying attributed to Katie G. Cannon, the progenitor of womanist theological ethics. She was the first Black woman ordained in the United Presbyterian Church and the first woman to earn a doctorate at Union Theological Seminary.

growling." Racial justice became a key issue for Middle Church when Treyvon Martin was killed. That justice work put her squarely in the Black Lives Matter Movement. Middle Church, like each ministry studied, is anti-racist and pro-LGBTQ, where all voices matter.

3. Communal Christology

A womanist ecclesiology is informed by a communal Christology. Jesus invited a community of men and women to follow him, learn from him, love one another, and then communicate that transformational love in the world. Dr. Melva Sampson and Pink Robe Chronicles (PRC) demonstrate this communal element each Sunday morning in their Cyber Assembly on Facebook Live. For Dr. Sampson, the PRC community preaches with her. For example, if she references a website or quote during her sermon but can't remember where it's located, someone from the PRC community finds it and posts it in the thread. Dr. Sampson, a homiletics professor and practical theologian, describes her sermon offering as an "active communal approach" to preaching and explains: "We all preach it together because they (PRC community) have an active role in it. It's not, 'This is what I came to give you'—it may start out that way, but the PRC community is like seasoning on food; they enhance whatever dish is being made by me."

4. Organically Trauma-Informed

"Trauma is an emotional wound resulting from a shocking event or multiple and repeated life-threatening experiences that may cause lasting negative effects on a person, disrupting the path of healthy physical, emotional, spiritual, and intellectual development."[17] At Rize Community Church, there are women who have been prostituted as well as members with histories of drug addiction. Dr. Handy and other ministry leaders understand the trauma that accompanies such histories and have created an environment where each person feels valued and is able to live authentically. Rize also has a large Black LGBTQIA young adult population, many of whom have been dislocated and disconnected from their families due to unhealthy theological and biblical perspectives.

There is also *cultural trauma* which occurs when "members of a collectivity feel they have been subjected to a horrendous event that

17. Liddle, "Trauma and Young Offenders," 5.

leaves indelible marks upon their group consciousness, marking their memories forever and changing their future identity in fundamental and irrevocable ways."[18] Black women live at the intersection of varied and multiple levels of trauma, such as race-based and gender-based discrimination and oppression. By virtue of Black women's lived experiences at the intersection of racial and gender-based trauma, a womanist ecclesiology speaks to the impact of that trauma on their relationships with other people and their understanding of God and spirituality. A womanist ecclesiology means womanist practitioners understand how vulnerable people are who have been traumatized and that their sense of safety can be triggered by any number of things. Most importantly, those who have been traumatized need to be encouraged and supported in being hopeful about their own healing and wholeness. Consequently, a trauma-informed approach to ministry asks and seeks to address the question, "What happened to you?" rather than "What did you do?" A womanist ecclesiology, as evidenced by all the ministries in Irie's study, is a conduit of healing and wholeness for humanity.

5. Universal God

A womanist ecclesiology is wide and broad enough to encompass a variety of spiritual and religious expressions. It sets forth that God is Spirit and cannot be contained, controlled, or confined. One of the most clarifying experiences of the universality of God occurred while Irie attended Sunday afternoon worship at Rize Community Church. Rize is a blending of Christianity and Ifá, a Yoruba religion originating in West Africa. This particular Sunday, Rize celebrated Pastor Regina Belle-Battle[19] with a Kwatakye award presentation. The Kwatakye is an African symbol for bravery, fearlessness, and valor. Kwatakye was a famous, fearless African warrior and captain. The manner in which the women of the congregation honored Pastor Belle-Battle was especially moving to Irie. They engaged in a naming and water ritual and presented Pastor Belle-Battle with a piece of kente cloth as a stole.

Similarly, Dr. Melva Sampson experiences God as Universal as she embraces an Afro-centered Christian spirituality. In a sermon

18. Alexander et al., "Toward a Theory of Cultural Trauma," 1.

19. Regina Bell-Battle is an R&B and Gospel recording artist. She and her husband co-pastor New Shield of Faith Church in Atlanta, Georgia. They provide nesting space for Rize Community Church.

preached at the Festival of Homiletics in Minneapolis, Minnesota, Dr. Sampson made the following assertion:

> I am unapologetically Afro-centric; I see myself in the words of Dr. Molefi Asante as a subject in a world, in a Christian tradition, and in a preaching praxis that so often objectify me. Hence, I illumine the history, the current experiences, and the hopes of African diasporan people in contrast to what is often posited from particular hegemonic, colonialist, and imperialist pulpits . . . I am also unapologetically a follower of Jesus.[20]

Upon hearing her words, those in attendance, particularly the Black clergywomen seated with and around Irie, erupted with thunderous applause. Dr. Sampson expressed in her sermon what all of them believed and have in one way or another claimed as true for themselves and their respective ministries—it is possible to mine the values, virtues, and culture of their African heritage and be followers of the life and teachings of Jesus Christ, all at the same time, because they believe they serve a Universal God. More specifically, Black Christian women who are clergy, social justice activists, preachers, biblical scholars, and theologians are finding healing and wholeness rooted in learning their ancestral African heritage and histories.

6. Womanist Preachers as Primary Proclaimers

In each of the ministries Irie explored, the primary preachers and proclaimers are womanist practitioners. Some are senior pastors with several paid staff members, as in the case of Dr. Jacqui Lewis and Dr. Maisha Handy. The word of liberation, transformation, and hope comes forth out of the mouths and bodies of Black clergywomen.

In making her way toward this revolutionary and transformational constructive framework, Irie found it helpful to reimagine Black women in terms of their embodiment. Specifically, she considered what it means to live, work, and carry out ministry in a Black female body, particularly when "the various ways in which black bodies are put upon by structures and ideologies of oppression land upon the black female body."[21] Malcolm X, during his iconic May 1962 speech

20. This quote was in the introduction of a sermon preached by Dr. Melva Sampson during the 2019 Festival of Homiletics in Minneapolis, Minnesota.

21. Douglas, *Black Bodies and the Black Church*, 35.

in Los Angeles, confirmed a truth about Black women's embodiment that most Black women, even to this day, resist internalizing: "The most disrespected woman in America is the black woman. The most un-protected person in America is the black woman. The most neglected person in America is the black woman."[22] As a consequence of this flagrant discounting and dehumanization, Black female bodies are not typically embraced or sought out in North American religious, theological, and ecclesial spaces as sites of knowledge production and socio-religious innovation and transformation. However, the North American church would do well to cease misinterpreting the Black female body. In order to accomplish such a paradigmatic shift, the North American church might reimagine the body of Jesus. That is, consider alternative theoretical models of incarnation. Here's what I mean: "Just as Jesus in-fleshed God, God is *in* the flesh of Black women as well."[23] Below, Marshall Turman articulates the idea of God *in* Black women's flesh, as a womanist ethic of the incarnation:

> Positing black women as Jesus, that is, as the image of God's ethical identity in the world, however, a womanist ethic of incarnation insists that the black church's parousia is possible only insofar as it remembers Jesus by looking to the bodies of black church women who, in their apparent brokenness, claim that God is not only *with* us in terms of God's presence in history on the side of the oppressed; but even more, God is *in* us, namely, that God is *in* the flesh of even the "oppressed of the oppressed."[24]

Funding

Irie discovered that, with the exception of Middle Collegiate Church, each ministry lacked denominational funding to support any of these Black clergywomen. They relied on offerings from the church, donations from the larger community, and various grants. Each of the Black clergywomen held a second conventional job or relied on speaking and teaching to augment their income.

22. Malcolm X, "Who Taught You to Hate Yourself?" para. 3.
23. Turman, *Toward a Womanist Ethic*, 172.
24. Turman, *Toward a Womanist Ethic*, 172.

In the case of The Gathering, A Womanist Church, the co-pastors received a New Church grant after being in ministry without compensation for eight months. This grant enabled them to split a very modest salary for a year and a half. At the writing of this book they have five months of grant money remaining, and do not know if the grant will renew. Whether it renews or not, The Gathering will continue listening to the Spirit and use creativity to develop strategies for economic thriving. The North American Church also has a responsibility and a challenge to provide strategies for these much-needed ministries to attain economic sustainability.

Guidance for Creating Womanist Churches

As Irie's study clearly demonstrated, many people are discovering the power of a womanist ecclesiology. A womanist ecclesiology empowers Black clergywomen to partner in shaping communities that resist white supremacist capitalist patriarchy and liberate the oppressed. Many people in our country and around the world are looking for places like The Gathering, a community fully practicing a womanist ecclesiology. There are millions of churches in the United States alone, but The Gathering is distinct as the only church founded and identified as a womanist church. The Gathering co-pastors and ministry partners hope to inspire the creation of many more womanist churches. They offer guidance for creating a womanist church:

1. Begin by praying about creating a womanist church. Planting a new church takes a great deal of work and commitment. Do not try to plant a womanist church just because it sounds good; plant a womanist church only if called to do it. Kamilah, Irie, and Yvette felt called to create The Gathering; they could no longer wait for others to give them space. They had to create the table where they wanted to sit.
2. Create a womanist church in partnership with others. The Gathering has been a model of partnership, begun intentionally with three Black clergywomen. Each wanted other gifted women to carry the load with her and to show the world that Black women can work together. In 2019, Yvette left The Gathering to work on food justice issues and other ministries in her denomination. Irie and Kamilah continue to co-pastor, believing this is the best model. They also work with ministry partners to fulfill the mission of The Gathering. They know that Jesus did not work alone, and neither should they.

3. Create a womanist church with clearly stated womanist beliefs and priorities, and stick to them. Stand strong in these beliefs to bring the vision to reality. When the co-pastors started The Gathering by stating social justice priorities of racial equity, LGBTQIA inclusion, and elimination of patriarchy, misogyny, and sexism (PMS), they knew they would turn many people away, but they took this stand anyway.
4. Be open to a variety of creative modes of worship and to diverse spiritual and religious expressions, and be artistically expressive in liturgies. Engage womanist preachers as the primary proclaimers, informed by Black women's experiences of trauma and resistance to oppression.
5. When creating a womanist church, define "success." For The Gathering, success did not mean having a big crowd of people, but helping to transform people and to create an equitable world.
6. Explore many funding options and develop creative strategies for the economic thriving of a womanist church. Listen to the Spirit and have faith in God's guidance.
7. Claim the vision of womanist churches bringing liberation and wholeness to all people. Believe that creating a womanist church will contribute to bringing this vision to reality in order to transform church and society.

3

Experiencing a Womanist Church

A WOMANIST CHURCH EMBODIES a collaborative leadership structure. Instead of "members," The Gathering, A Womanist Church has "ministry partners," designating their participation together to fulfill the prophetic mission of the church. Partnership in ministry gives people a deeper sense of belonging and connection in the faith community. Ministry partners use their gifts, voices, networks, and platforms in working together toward their liberating, transformative vision of justice and wholeness for all people.

This song, sung at The Gathering, celebrates the communal ministry of a womanist church.

All Together We Have Power[1]
(sung to the tune of "Every Time I Feel the Spirit")

Refrain:
All together we have power,
rising up against all the wrong;
all together we have power,
rising up to sing freedom songs.

The Spirit in us feels so strong,
giving us hope to labor long. (Refrain)

When we are stifled and oppressed,
we will all share our deep distress. (Refrain)

1. Aldredge-Clanton, "All Together We Have Power," 20–21.

When things around us don't feel right,
we will resist with all our might. (Refrain)

The Spirit in all brings new birth,
moving with love through all the earth. (Refrain)

In this chapter, ministry partners tell their experiences of The Gathering, A Womanist Church. The chapter begins with the story of Rev. Winner A. Laws, who started her journey with The Gathering as a ministry partner and later became minister of congregational care and spiritual support.

Rev. Winner A. Laws

The Making of a Womanist Preacher

Am I a Womanist?

In March of 2016, Rev. Dr. Irie Session and I were on a panel titled "Black Women Symposium: Race, Gender, and Sexuality" at the African American Museum in Dallas, Texas. We started to talk in the "mingle" room prior to the event. She began to ask me questions about my background and my goals in life. I shared with her that I was graduating from Texas Christian University's Brite Divinity School. I wanted to use my acquired knowledge, as a Black lesbian Christian, to educate Black LGBTQIA+ people by using Scripture to support my theological perspective and show them that God loves them unconditionally. We had a very good conversation that evening about professional careers, Brite Divinity, and sexual orientation.

I learned a great deal about her during the symposium that evening, and I had the audacious idea that it would be great for Rev. Dr. Irie to preach at my home church, Cathedral of Hope United Church of Christ (UCC), at some point in the future. I heard that she was putting together a Good Friday Worship Service focused on the Seven Last Words of Jesus from the cross[2] with only Black women preaching. The particular Black

2. The Seven Last Words or Seven Last Sayings of Christ Good Friday Service is a tradition in the Black Church that brings together the community to commemorate the final words of Jesus Christ while nailed to the cross. Seven preachers, typically men, proclaim the Seven Last Sayings spoken by Jesus Christ from the cross.

women to preach were self-identified as womanist. This meant sermons were to be preached through the lens of womanist biblical interpretation. I enthusiastically informed my peers about the event, and we attended the church service that evening. We were totally captivated as we listened to these seven women preach the word of God. This phenomenal spiritual service motivated me to work with the Cathedral of Hope UCC senior pastor to have Dr. Irie as our guest preacher for the Sunday morning Juneteenth services in June 2017.

Dr. Irie shared a word from God at both the 9:00 a.m. and 11:00 a.m. services to celebrate Juneteenth. The way she preached both inspired and spiritually moved me as well as the congregation. They were talking about and recommending her sermon for the next ninety days. I began to research more intently the definition of "womanist theology." I was intrigued that her preaching style included womanist theology because it was so vibrant and real; I could relate to it personally. The experience made me wonder, "Am I Womanist Preacher?" I had just been certified as a licensed minister by the UCC denomination, so I knew I would have to preach in order to be ordained.

I was then motivated to purchase a book by Kimberly P. Johnson titled *The Womanist Preacher*. She explained in detail the definition of "womanism" and the womanist tenets including radical subjectivity, traditional communalism, redemptive self-love, and critical engagement. She also included several womanist sermons. As I studied and listened to more womanist preachers over the next year, I decided that this most closely matched my theological belief system because it included me as a Black woman who was gay and wanted to use Scripture to share God's unconditional love for everyone, regardless of race, sexual orientation, class, and gender. I wanted to be a womanist preacher.

What Does It Mean to Be a Womanist Preacher?

As a result of my experience with the Seven Last Words sermons and Kimberly P. Johnson's book, I found several other womanist preachers who had written books related to womanist biblical hermeneutics. Delores S. Williams's *Sisters in the Wilderness: The Challenge of Womanist God-Talk*, Renita J. Weems's *Just a Sister Away: A Womanist Vision of Women's Relationships in the Bible*, and Mitzi J. Smith's *I Found God in Me: A Womanist Biblical Hermeneutics Reader*—I could add these books to my collection of theological resources. Dr. Irie Session also held a conference in May of 2016 titled "The Theresa Fry Brown Women's Preaching and Leadership Institute," and she invited me to attend. I repeatedly declined, because I felt like I was not a preacher. She reassured me that the conference was for all people who wanted to learn more about womanism and that anyone could attend. I was fascinated about the guest speakers as well as the classes that were offered, so I signed up and attended. The conference was a success, and I was very glad that I attended. I learned more about the definition and origin of womanism, and hopes for the future to help more Black women to have a place, a home in the pulpit, sharing the word of God.

Historically in the Black church, men were ministers and pastors; women had limited opportunity to preach. Patriarchy confined the pulpit to men. The gospel was therefore preached through the narrow and oppressive lens of patriarchy. On the other hand, Rev. Irie's goal and vision was for anointed women to know that their voice as preachers and ministers was also a divine call from God. The Teresa Fry Brown Institute was created to give women the support and the tools to help them be more successful in following their divine call. Every time I heard women like Rev. Irie preach, it resonated in my spirit and my soul. I continued to believe that there should be more women preachers in the pulpit and that God authorizes them to preach.

I love the idea and the reality of using Black women's narratives, and I love to hear our ancestor's voices and experiences as part of a sermon. I know how my mother, grandmothers, aunts, and other Black women experienced life, church, and community. Their statements of faith were not just talk; they were "tried and true" as they related to their cultural and gender experiences. They are my first personal examples of true "womanism," even though the term was not defined during those years. Hearing womanist preachers using womanist rhetoric and bringing the stories of Hagar, Rahab, Jesus' mother Mary, Mary Magdalene, Esther, and Priscilla to life is spiritually moving. It is captivating and soul-stirring to hear the womanist preachers' exploration of ethical issues as they relate to our salvation.

Kimberly P. Johnson writes, "Redemptive self-love sermons focus on self-love, but they also lift up the fact that the biblical character already loves herself enough to resist being silenced or losing her dignity or self-worth . . . a woman in a redemptive self-love sermon already loves herself regardless."[3] This quote connects with my spirit and soul because I know that God created me. As a Black lesbian Christian woman, I too refuse to be silenced about my sexual orientation. I know God loves me because She created me, and I love myself enough to know that my dignity and self-worth have never been in question because I know God knows everything about me. I feel affirmed and compelled to tell others in the community (traditional communalism) through womanist preaching of God's unconditional love for us all.

My Womanist Journey—A Revelation of Good News

On Saturday, October 14, 2017, The Gathering held their first worship service. I was there in the front row, eager to hear a word from God. I continued to attend these services, and during my theological reflections I would be motivated to study the Bible to see how my life, my history, and my stories related to the biblical stories. As I worked with my appointed spiritual director to determine if I were being called by God to be an ordained minister, we used the story in the Bible of "The Samaritan Woman at the Well" (John 4:4–42).

My cultural and religious experiences conveyed that women should not be allowed behind the pulpit; therefore, my embedded theology was that a woman should not preach. As a Black woman who grew up in a patriarchal family, I heard repeatedly, through the words of my Baptist preachers and my family, that women had no place in the pulpit. It took a great deal of deconstructing, self-reflection, prayer, and meditation for me to come to realize the call on my life to share the word of God from any pulpit in any theological form and then to become a womanist preacher.

I am called and anointed to let other people know of God's grace, forgiveness, and unconditional love. Womanism helps me live into my call in ways that are authentic and unique to my identity as a Black lesbian Christian preacher. On one occasion during a time of meditation, the Holy Spirit affirmed my call to preach. I was led to read and study Acts 1:8: "But you will receive power when the Holy Spirit has come upon you; and you will be my witnesses in Jerusalem, in all Judea and Samaria, and to the ends of the earth." I have been preaching and getting feedback from pastors and ministers, helping to pull the stories about women and their contribution to the forefront of my sermons. I am also interviewing my relatives and friends

3. Johnson, *The Womanist Preacher*, 75.

to add to my collection of relatable stories. Womanism gives voice to Black women's experiences as they relate to our cultural and social constructs. It also gives voice to spirituality, family, and community practices that have for centuries been curated by Black women from all over the world.

The wisdom and the knowledge being shared through womanist preaching is life-affirming and liberating. When preparing for sermons, I want to add womanist quotes and stories to my sermons that are relatable and pertinent to the sermon's focus and biblical text. For example, in January of 2020 I preached a sermon titled "Infinite Possibilities," and my Scripture reference was Psalms 98. Here is an excerpt from that sermon:

> When we look at this passage, we see that the promise of salvation, steadfast love, faith, and justice includes the environment. We have some ecological turmoil that is evident by some of the things happening in our weather today. Womanist theologian Melanie L. Harris writes, "just as women of color have often survived multiple forms of oppression when confronting racism, classism, sexism, and heterosexism, androcentric attitudes devaluing the earth and privileging (particular) humans over the earth's well-being have resulted in the environmental crisis in which we all find ourselves."[4] Tornadoes in December in Texas, Australia fires, longer wildfire seasons, stronger hurricanes than ever before. In fact, global warming is seen as one of the top threats in the world today; however, there is little action to slow down the direction or to help stop the trend. This does not spell good news for future generations to have clean air, clean water, or a planet that is devoid of toxins. The plants, the animals, and all of the earth are at risk.

When first studying and reflecting on Psalms 98 while preparing for the sermon, I recognized that it had several ecological implications that could be researched, and I also recognized that Melanie L. Harris specialized in ecowomanism. I knew her work could add value to my sermon from a womanist perspective.

The Gathering, A Womanist Church in Dallas, Texas

In the spring of 2018, I recognized that The Gathering, A Womanist Church had three cisgender co-pastors, so I called Rev. Irie and asked if they would consider adding me to their staff. I made this request as I was about to

4. Harris, "Ecowomanism: An Introduction," 6.

be ordained. The ministry partners who regularly attended our services were approximately 50 percent LGBTQIA+, and I believed it would be beneficial to have someone on staff who identified as non-cisgender. I was interviewed and asked how I could contribute to The Gathering's ministry by the co-pastors. I shared my vision of supporting educational programs, congregational care activities, and preaching about pertinent LGBTQIA+ topics to which all ministry partners could relate.

When it was time for me to be ordained, I wanted a womanist preacher to share the gospel message to the congregation and ministry partners. I asked Rev. Irie to preach my ordination service, using John 4:4–42. I knew it would be different for my family to hear a woman preacher because they believe in the tradition of having men as preachers. I do not believe that they had ever heard a woman preach. I wanted my ordination to be the first time for them, since this was such a significant milestone in my spiritual journey. It was a great service despite the weather challenges of the day. We had more than 125 people in the Cathedral of Hope UCC–Interfaith Peace Chapel. The inclement weather caused a power outage. There was no electricity, and the ceremony was performed without lights, microphones, or air conditioning. The June heat was challenging. But it was truly a womanist service. With the sunlight beaming in through the windows, I was ordained by the grace of God. It was not lost on me or others who attended the service how we were spiritually blessed by the womanist preaching, the gospel music, and the whole ordination ceremony.

The entire church benefited from participating in the ordination service by hearing a message of community involvement, justice, critical engagement, radical subjectivity, and self-love. My family, friends, ministry partners, Cathedral of Hope UCC church members, and I were blessed by the womanist message "Because of Who You Are" by Rev. Dr. Irie Session. Rev. Kamilah Hall Sharp, co-pastor of The Gathering, led the presentation portion of my ordination service. Many of The Gathering ministry partners were present to lay hands on me in support of my ordination. I was ecstatic to have a new place to call my spiritual home.

Now I am an ordained United Church of Christ minister of congregational care and spiritual support at The Gathering, A Womanist Church. As a womanist preacher, I am committed to sharing narratives of Black women's experiences to empower all people spiritually and to be a voice for those on the margins to find their place in the creation story.

The Gathering, A Womanist Church

Phil Lucia

I first heard about womanism from Hebrew Bible Professor Wil Gafney, when she was a guest on "The Bible For Normal People" podcast. I began following her on Twitter, and later saw a tweet about her preaching at The Gathering, A Womanist Church one weekend in 2017. I had no idea then that she was based in the Dallas-Fort Worth area nor that a womanist church was within driving distance from me. Although I didn't make it to hear her preach that weekend, I resolved to visit The Gathering at my earliest opportunity to see the church for myself.

Having become interested in liberation theologies broadly through personal study following my deconstruction of my own white American evangelicalism, I was primed and ready for the experience of The Gathering, A Womanist Church. There I found the message of womanism in particular both compelling and the right kind of mystifying.

As a straight white man, I'm accustomed to theologies crafted by and for people who look like me and who've experienced the world with the wind at our backs, so learning about the development of an entire school of theology made explicitly by and for people whose experiences I did not share and could not intuit was intriguing enough on its own. Add in the rich theological and societal vision that womanists bring to the Christian conversation, and I was keenly interested in reading and learning more. When I eventually discovered that such an opportunity existed "in the real world" outside my books and Twitter feed, and only a 40-minute drive from my front door, I felt I simply had to go and witness it firsthand.

When I first attended The Gathering, I noticed that the community was smaller than I had expected. I didn't realize how new the church still was at that point, and figured that the offer of in-person womanist preaching (and from such gifted speakers) would surely be bringing the crowds. I also noticed and appreciated the racial mix of the congregants after my recent experiences in the suburbs attending lily-white mainline churches. But honestly, at first I felt a little bit unsure and intimidated to walk into a place that was so upfront about existing for and uplifting people who weren't like me. Would I be welcomed, or mistrusted? Could I listen and learn without getting offended or being blamed? In short—was I safe?

These were among my first such feelings of misgiving walking into any new church, and while the folks at The Gathering couldn't have been more gracious or friendly to me, that's not always the outcome when those same feelings are experienced by women, Black/Indigenous/people-of-color, and

LGBTQ+ people walking into the sorts of churches where I had previously belonged. Real harm is done in pulpits and pews across the world when racism, patriarchy, misogyny, and sexism are preached as the will of God.

None of these risks were mine to bear personally because of my identity. And I had been walking a path of seeking solidarity and identification with the marginalized enough to recognize that The Gathering stood an excellent chance of being a safe place for any person still willing to part the doors of a brick-and-mortar church to attend a service.

Finally, I was impressed by a feeling of abundance in this little church body. While The Gathering is not numerically large, the theology and liturgy of the church reinforced an impression of "enoughness" to which I still feel strongly drawn. This seems like nothing less than a small taste of the abundance of the coming kin-dom[5] of heaven.

The Gathering has been a true community to me. I've had life-changing conversations, made friends, been carried through hard times, been inspired, found God, and more—on a weekly basis. There's always a reason to show up early and stay late, and my six-year-old son looks forward to coming as much as I do.

The opportunity to hear from different gifted preachers on a regular rotating basis is such a gift! They bring thoughtful and impassioned engagement with texts and theologies to their sermons—this is unmatched in my church experiences, either in the evangelical or Protestant mainline world. And the routine invitation to "Talk Back to the Text" invites a reflective, contemplative listening that never fails to elicit both gratitude for the sermon and preacher, and further probing questions that strengthen the community by their airing. There is a rare and sacred atmosphere that takes hold after the preacher momentarily sits and the congregation is invited to reflect on the sermon and text—a serious but never oppressive collective inhalation and exhalation of inspiration foreshadowing a thoughtful communal examination of themes.

With time and repetition, this straight white man has come to understand better that the vision of womanism includes healing and wholeness for all people of any racial identity, of any or no gender, of any or no sexuality. Womanism generously invites all kinds of people to share in the

5. The word "kin-dom" is an inclusive alternative to "kingdom"; "kin-dom" emphasizes the nonsexist, nonclassist nature of God's realm and underscores our common kinship with God and one another.

abundance that follows from giving Black women the power and authority they are properly due.

Because I felt welcomed into a wonderful, vibrant stream of people moving in the same direction to create a world of righteousness/justice and true equity, I became a ministry partner in The Gathering. Being part of something I believe is so important for healing the world is a privilege and a challenge worth striving for. The requirements for ministry partnership (vocalizing, attendance, giving, sharing of talents) were perfectly in line with what I was prepared to do once I found a place as unique and vital as The Gathering. And I appreciated the pastors' partnership in promptly completing the Verified Clear survey from ChurchClarity.com, another organization I work with doing important work to push the church universal toward treating all people with honesty and respect.

The Gathering has given me a place to grow and express my convictions; a community to help me endure through and heal after some of the toughest experiences of my life; a launch point for involvement in activism, politics, and advocacy; and a safe space to feel the warmth of God's motherly presence. In short, it's been a source of consistency, trust, opportunity, deep thought, challenge, laughter, and joy.

To unpack that some, I need to discuss where I've come from. I needed a place of healing from some of my previous experiences in non-LGBTQ-affirming and non-egalitarian white evangelical churches—churches where God's voice was constrained and warped through lenses of heteronormative purity culture and pastoral ego, where Black voices were scarce and filtered specifically for their willingness not to challenge the white faith consensus, where emotions were treated as distractions at best and a source of demonic influence at worst, where the flourishing of people was subordinate to the strength-over of the church corporate and the small tyranny of quantity over quality, where the longest-tenured members resembled Christ the least. To put a finer point on it, the 2016 election and subsequent geopolitical events have laid bare many of the failings of the white evangelical church in America. I think I understand some of what Reggie Williams meant when he wrote: "Although the pro-Nazi Christians of the German Christian movement and his colleagues of the Confessing Church movement understood themselves to be faithful Christians, Bonhoeffer had identified lethal problems within their Christianity. Like American pro-segregation Christians, the pro-Nazi German Christians demonstrated in a negative way that the mere claim to be a Christian is not an indication of faithful discipleship; what matters is one's interpretation of Christlikeness, how one interprets the way of Jesus."[6]

My faith, which once had withered on the vine through my own neglect brought on by my skepticism of churches and the impact on their members, has now never been stronger because of the consistent community and theological depth and diversity of the preachers and people alongside my son and me in the pews of The Gathering. I can always walk into church knowing that I'll be welcomed, and I'll be fed by nourishing thoughts and examples of faithful spiritual giants, where emulating Jesus is the ultimate goal and not toeing the line or falling into conformity. Like the experience of my personal hero Bonhoeffer at Abyssinian Baptist Church in Harlem, my immersion in a different form of Christian faith has revolutionized the way I hear and follow Christ.

My vision is for The Gathering to continue to grow and reach more willing participants, but trusting that it will be the right size for the point in time that we're at and that the quality of engagement in the life of the church will always take priority over the quantity of attendees. As the message is preached and lived, it will and must reach a growing number of people both like and unlike me, hungry for a flowering spiritual life but dissatisfied and knowing something is missing in the forms of church they've been handed.

I acknowledge that my own vision is limited. My inherent biases are always going to be with me in some form, try as I might to educate them toward mitigation. But I can continue to show up with an intentional stance of humility and openness, to trust the pastors and leaders of The Gathering to set our direction toward where our collective care and attention can do the most good.

Welcoming and getting to know one another by name and story is vital to a healthy church community. I hope to increase the depth and number of the friendships I've made at our weekly "Greet & Tweet" and unofficial after-service chats.

Being a natural problem solver, I intend to watch carefully as the ministry of The Gathering adapts to changing times and circumstances, and offer my talent, time, and treasure to aid in whatever ministry areas I can. In short, I aim to increase my own involvement in ways that benefit our Gathering community while preserving my own health (because self-care is a necessary part of doing justice work—thanks, womanism) and stretching

6. Williams, *Bonhoeffer's Black Jesus*, 3.

my outlook and experiences to accommodate whatever the coming years hold for Dallas, for Texas, for the U.S., and for the world.

Vontril McLemore

In early October of 2019, I was watching TV and saw a memorial prayer vigil for the late Botham Jean, the young Black man who was murdered in his home by a white female police officer while sitting on his couch eating ice cream. I noticed a beautiful Black woman at the podium praying, a statuesque, magnificent Sistah replete with a coiffured, fiery red Afro. I discovered she was part of the cadre of community activists—clergymen/women, government officials, attorneys and citizens—who were celebrating the life of Mr. Jean. To my utter surprise and amazement, I discovered the Afrocentric woman praying was a minister, and her name was Rev. Dr. Irie Session!

Also in attendance were Mr. Jean's mother and other family members. The poise and dignity of the Rev. Dr. Session was very elegant, comforting, and confident, but not arrogant. I thought, "hmmmmmm, this is interesting," and it definitely piqued my interest. The day prior to seeing the vigil, I had poured my heart out to a friend and prayer warrior about my concern that my daughter may never find a place of worship that suited her. Imagine my shock and awe seeing Dr. Session less that twenty-four hours later! Indeed, the Scripture says, "Seek first the [kin-dom] of God . . . , and all these [blessings] shall be added to you" (Matthew 6:33 NKJV). Hallelujah!

My first experience of The Gathering, A Womanist Church, on October 19, 2019, was overwhelmingly soul edifying, powerful, empowering, full of hope and forgiveness and reconciliation. Dr. Session taught on biblical reconciliation, and I was an attentive student (when the student is ready, the teacher will appear)! I was sitting on the edge of my seat, hanging onto her every word. Her message caught and kept my attention. I remember her stating that forgiveness without reconciliation is not correct biblical doctrine, as they are components of the same theology. Forgiveness is often predicated on the powerless in communities habitually being exploited and minimized amidst the unequal power structure, invariably enabling those in power to continue detrimental activities, without recompense or restoration or reconciliation, in our communities of color. Our communities are continuously traumatized and left on our own to deal with the consequences of being traumatized.

Dr. Session also challenged us with the following query: how can an unjust system render a just verdict? I couldn't believe my ears. It had been decades since I had heard such a dynamic, thought-provoking, pragmatic, and honest examination of the systems we depend on for our very life, liberty, and happiness. It was truly *revolutionary*!

When I came through the door of the church that houses The Gathering, I remember uttering these words, "I was not aware that such an animal existed, the likes of which I've never seen before!" Those were my true feelings about coming into The Gathering. Having just seen the movie *Harriet,* I found The Gathering especially powerful. As Dr. Session talked about forgiveness, she quoted Botham Jean's mother: "I don't want to see just anything; I want to see something more." The teaching by Dr. Session that night was something that I had not heard since the sixties when I was listening to the civil rights ministers as they preached, sang, and suffused Christianity with the true meaning of social justice, mercy, equality, and equity. As my daughter says, I was "blown away." I was flummoxed. I did not realize that I needed this Gathering experience. Had my daughter not refused to attend the traditional evangelical church that we'd been members of for the last fifteen years, I would have had no reason to even pursue finding a church like The Gathering.

I grew up in a Southern Baptist tradition where Black male pastors preached the word. They were fiery rhetoricians. They were oratorical Titans and Giants. On the other hand, the women were always relegated to subservient helper roles. These positions were oftentimes the musicians, the baby sitters, coordinators of pastors' teas, and the like. At The Gathering it was so edifying for me to see scholarly, wise, and emboldened women crossing the border. Unapologetically Black women speaking truth to power from the pulpit was unbelievable. Another component of The Gathering that astounded me was the participation of white women who are supporters of womanist philosophy.

Whereas my soul was finally at rest and felt complete, as if the missing link was no longer missing, I felt compelled to become a ministry partner. I wanted to give of my talent, time, and treasure to further the mission of The Gathering: to diagnose, remedy, and heal from the ravages of patriarchy, misogyny, and sexism (PMS) by replacing them with womanist ideology that empowers women, thus trickling to the entire community. I have finally found a church that both my daughter and I can sit side by side in again.

We are welcomed to utilize our power and gifts without compromising our culture and beliefs, and without being invisible, as Ralph Ellison[7] wrote.

When we attended the traditional evangelical church, I was told that I possibly would have been unable to wear my scarf on my head for the Christmas musical. This hurt my heart, especially after faithfully dedicating my time, talent, and treasure for the past fifteen years at my previous church. I was crushed. The church boasts 187 countries, several of them formerly Muslims. Again, the philosophy of assimilation was assumed. I was told that the ministers had to confer to decide how much diversity they required of the choir members. When did "come as you are" get replaced by a quota system?

I shared that experience with The Gathering, and immediately the ministry partners took me to their bosoms. They prayed with me and assured me that I have a place in their choir anytime I want to sing, scarf and all! I've now become a member of The Gathering's worship team. Thank you "traditional" church for letting me down, because had you not, I would not have found The Gathering. Scripture states, "All things work together for good for those . . . who are called according to God's purpose" (Romans 8:28). Obviously, this was indeed God's plan for me to find The Gathering.

Dr. Session preached a sermon titled "Rock Steady," in which she taught, reinforced, and punctuated the need for all Black women in their communities to be consistent with their time, talent, and treasure, and reliable in our support of the causes that will uplift, empower, eradicate trauma, and restore our communities. She gave me a diagnosis, a treatment plan, tools, goals, and objectives to aid in this endeavor. The Gathering voices societal ills and provides remedies for them as well.

As I listened to Rev. Kamilah Hall Sharp with her womanist sass, I realized that I needed to cross the border as Jesus' family crossed the border from Israel to Egypt to flee the persecution of the horrific King Herod in order for the Messiah to be born free from harassment and persecution. The Gathering made the transition seamless and enabled me to make my border-crossing from the "traditional evangelical congregation" to the revolutionary Gathering experience. Crossing over the border from invisibility. Crossing over from apathy. Crossing the border from cultural ignorance. Crossing the border from stagnation, disengagement from the policies that hurt people of color. Crossing the border from soul destroying to soul engagement and empowerment!

7. Ellison, *Invisible Man.*

Elizabeth Barrett Browning wrote, "How do I love thee? Let me count the ways."[8] I love The Gathering, a remarkable one-of-a-kind worship experience. The Gathering has changed my life and the life of my daughter, which changes my life. My daughter had not attended church regularly for about two years. Our church disappointed her tremendously, not intentionally, but by sheer ignorance. Henceforth, she said she cannot attend there anymore, and now we're sitting side by side in a church that checked every block of her worship wish list and more. Her dad and I would question her about what kind of church would get her back in the pews. The list that she gave was unattainable, or so I thought. Her dad finally asked her a couple weeks before we were made aware of The Gathering, "I think you want to attend a church that has an activist leaning." Her response was, "Yes! That's it! That's what I want!" The Gathering offers a spiritual outlet, and it also prioritizes activism and outreach to the community.

On February 16, 2020, I brought my three grandsons to The Gathering as well. It is incredibly important to introduce our young Black males to the value of women teaching and preaching, honoring their inherent existence. To recognize the dignity and virtue of women not as just sexual beings but as queens worthy of respect is very important to me.

My vision is for The Gathering to be replicated worldwide, to be self-sustaining, and to continue to empower those who have been left out, made invisible, ostracized, and criticized due to their intersectional diversity. In a sermon at The Gathering titled "Infinite Possibilities: Psalm 98:3–6," Rev. Winner Laws used the analogy of gumbo to demonstrate Christ's design for humanity. The ingredients for the gumbo are as varied and diverse as there are species of flowers on the planet. There is no one way to make gumbo; however, the purists would vehemently disagree. The variety and diversity in all God's creations are to be celebrated and not disregarded as insignificant. If one listens carefully, you can hear the whole earth giving praise to God. The sea, the fish, and the wind howl in majestically baritone harmonies. Should we be relegated to less than that in our worship of God? No way!

Luke 4:18–19 epitomizes The Gathering's ministry: "The Spirit of the Lord is upon me. She has anointed me to preach the good news to the poor. She has sent me to heal the brokenhearted. To proclaim liberty to the captives and recovery of sight to the blind. To set at liberty those who are oppressed. To proclaim the acceptable year of the Lord" (author paraphrase).

8. Browning, "How Do I Love Thee?"

These are my goals and aspirations for The Gathering, that more men and women of all stripes—all genders, classes, cultures—be afforded the opportunity to attend a worship service where all are truly welcome at this table. When she leads Communion at The Gathering, Rev. Winner Laws states: "This isn't my table; this isn't the church's table; this is God's table and all are welcome!"

Alexandria McLemore

I heard about The Gathering through my amazing mom. One day when I was at work, I received a text message from my mom, stating that she'd found a womanist church. Before I even finished reading my mom's text message, my immediate reaction was shock and complete disbelief. I previously attended a "traditional" evangelical church with which I later became disillusioned. Consequently, I never even allowed myself to imagine that such a place as The Gathering existed anywhere in the U.S., let alone in the South.

As I finished reading her text, I learned that my mother was watching a prayer vigil in honor of the late Botham Jean, and she saw Rev. Dr. Irie Session preaching and praying during the vigil. My mom texted that she googled Rev. Dr. Session, and The Gathering's website popped up. My mom clicked on their website and was blown away by their sermons. She suggested that we attend The Gathering that very same week.

When I clicked on The Gathering's website link, which was included in my mom's text message, I too was amazed. I was pleasantly surprised to learn that The Gathering had not one . . . not two . . . but three co-pastors who were all Black women! Additionally, I was pleased to learn that The Gathering hosts other African American women as guest pastors. I was so pleased that I agreed with my mom that we should attend The Gathering that week.

As a Black woman myself, I couldn't help but feel compelled to attend The Gathering. I was just so excited to become a part of a spiritual community in which I felt truly represented. After I stopped attending my former church, I practically gave up on finding a spiritual home that prioritized social justice, equity, and a space for women of color to access leadership positions in church.

Also, there was a little part of me who wanted to try another church at least once for my parents. My parents were very concerned about the fact that I stopped attending church for almost two years. Although my father tried not to express his concern, I could sense that both of my parents wanted to see me at least try once more to find a church home. I'm so glad I decided to attend The Gathering!

My first impression of The Gathering, A Womanist Church was literally, "Wow!" I was immediately excited when Rev. Dr. Session read the definition of "womanism." As a womanist myself, I wholeheartedly believe in the womanist tenants of spiritual activism, equity, and justice, and I was thrilled that The Gathering was spreading the virtues of womanism with other parishioners. Also, I was very proud to participate in a litany which provided visibility to the grave injustices of violence against women. Afterward, one the pastors delivered a rousing sermon, and I felt energized in my womanist ideology, ready to face another week. As my mom and I sat in my car after church, we both knew that we had found our new spiritual home.

As I have continued to participate in The Gathering, I have never felt more affirmed in a spiritual dwelling in my entire life. Every single aspect of my personhood as a Black woman is continually rendered visible each week at The Gathering. Having Black women leading a womanist church in a white supremacist, sexist society is inspirational, aspirational, and subversive. Each church service I'm revived with a renewed sense of self and my role within the overall liberation of marginalized people.

I became a ministry partner in The Gathering in order to give back to the community, and attempt in a small way to repay The Gathering pastors for the impact that they've made in my life. In my previous, more traditional church, I never felt comfortable participating in church activities. I didn't feel as if I could contribute anything to my previous church.

However, since joining The Gathering a couple of months ago, I started singing in the choir with my mother, collaborating with another ministry partner on creating short presentations during Black History Month about civil rights activists, and assisting Pastor Winner Laws with some research for one of her sermons. I've never been as involved in a church as I have been with The Gathering. It's as if I'm a completely new person. I'm so blessed to be a part of a revolutionary, spiritual movement.

The Gathering has reignited my passion for spiritual engagement and activism. The Gathering has also inspired me to continue to make space for my voice to be heard in society. For the first time in my life, I feel as if my presence is valued and treated as vital to the overall success of a church.

My vision is for The Gathering to continue to be a revolutionary, spiritual community of powerful people who prioritize social justice and center the struggles of people on the margins in society. I also envision The Gathering continuing to invite more people to become ministry partners and assist with the growth and overall success of our community.

Nommo Kofi Diop

My story of becoming active in The Gathering begins with my family background. My mother, who grew up in Mississippi, raised me in San Francisco along with my three sisters and two brothers. For sixty-two years she was married to my father, who worked for the police department and was rarely ever home. My mother was the nurturer, so I became close to her during my growing up years.

My mother was always involved in the PTA (Parent-Teacher Association) during my school years. During the time I was growing up, the PTA was a very racist organization. Usually made up of white women, the PTA never really gave my mother any role as a leader. But if they needed some cookies, she could definitely bring them cookies. I remember her telling me these stories, but it didn't deter her from being actively involved in my childhood education. She took education very seriously. She wanted us to be the best we possibly could be. Even though she had six children, she raised us as individuals.

When I was out of high school, she became a business owner. For more than ten years she ran a daycare and took care of other children in our home in San Francisco. I believe that if she hadn't had six children, she might have done even more. She had an ability to take care of finances, she had an ability to organize, and she had an ability to lead that everyone admired, whether it be in her church or her civic organizations or social organizations. My mother had an angelic personality. She was always smiling, always greeting folk, and always of service. I have admired my mother tremendously. She always came through for me. She traveled the world. She saw Europe and Africa, and she had an extensive reading collection. She was also a very thoughtful person when it came to social, civic, economic, and political events. After I graduated from college, we had many discussions about the world we lived in.

My mother's mother, who lived to be 102, was also a great influence on my life. My grandmother also was a businesswoman; she had a nursing home in her home. She had a long history of fighting the city of San Francisco to keep her property, and she was also a member of the Universal Negro Improvement Association. My grandmother was very proud of her accomplishments and of her ability to manage her life as much as she could while she was able. Then she was instrumental in making sure that my mother took care of her for the remainder of her life. Once my mother reached an age when I felt that this was very difficult for her, I helped take care of my grandmother. For about twenty years I was driving, shopping, cleaning, and doing all sorts of things to help my mother take care of my grandmother.

When I got married and had children, my wife and I became very active in our own children's lives in school. I joined the PTA. During that time there were very few men involved in PTA; predominantly women ran the organization. Also there were not a lot of Black people, so I became somewhat of an exceptional person in the PTA. I rose to the level of president of the high school PTA, went on to become the district president, and also worked at the state level. I shared my experiences in PTA with my mother. Our experiences were very similar. Even though I had leadership roles, I was serving cookies too. Whenever I tried to push the envelope or try to make a difference in the perception of African children in the public school system, there was always a lot of pushback and always a lot of racist tendencies being practiced.

My experiences of being involved as a parent I attribute to how my mother raised me to put children first. As a parent raising two sons and two daughters in San Francisco, I believed that going to church was important. My wife came from a Baptist tradition, and I came from a more nondenominational tradition of Christianity. We kept our children in church for the majority of their childhood. We joined the church that I grew up in when we got married but when our children reached their teenage years, we went to another nondenominational, evangelistic church. Later I went to a social justice church, Friendship-West Baptist Church, here in Dallas that aligned to my beliefs of African identity and African personality, and my wife went to a Pentecostal church.

Through my education and study of art I have developed a new sense of what it means to be a man. I have spent forty years painting and drawing, incorporating ideas into my artwork from reading African history and African beliefs. I also believe that I have been poisoned by this society, so I do not believe that in any way, shape, or form that I do not carry toxic male tendencies. It is impossible for me to live in a society that is so filled with racist, sexist, and capitalist ideologies to walk away from it without being damaged in the process. As a result of my upbringing and my belief in the future, I do believe that my thinking has been reorganized. Very few people I come in contact with would like to change the situation that we're living in.

I heard about The Gathering from Dr. Irie Session. I first met her at a Sunday morning service where she was preaching on a biblical text about a woman who saved her people from destruction. Her sermon was titled "Not Up in Here!" I was impressed with how she told the story and how if it weren't for this woman, the people would have been killed. At that service she said that the following Monday night she would be in the church to have a "Talk Back to the Text." There I learned more about early Christianity, how early Christianity was interpreted by toxic male leadership and a lot of the early Christian so-called "fathers" had a very toxic male mentality in their writing and interpretation of the text. I believe after I heard that, I needed to go hear the preaching at The Gathering. Since I started going, I have not stopped going, and I've been impressed by the stories told each Saturday by women preaching and by the discussions of the Bible from a womanist point of view.

The Gathering is different from other churches I've attended. The sermon is usually only about fifteen minutes, and the service lasts for no more than an hour. As a result, the message is more specific and focused. I appreciate the amount of time and energy Dr. Irie and Rev. Kamilah put into preparing messages and the different points of view of two women pastors. Hearing other women preachers has also been a good thing. Not only Rev. Kamilah and Rev. Irie, but many other Black women have brought messages at The Gathering in the same tone and in the same fashion with a different twist.

Another thing I like about The Gathering is "Talk Back to the Text," being able to discuss the Bible after the sermon. This was new for me. It gave me an opportunity to give my point of view of the sermon and is one of the main reasons that I attend The Gathering. It gives me an opportunity to engage with the preachers on the topic in a way that I relate to or the way I perceive it. It's good to hear other points of view and be able to share my point of view.

I became a ministry partner in The Gathering because I believe in the ideas that the women preachers are professing about God. I support this ministry because I want more people to hear these messages. I hope that through listening to these women preachers more people will come to realize the importance of doing away with systems like capitalism, racism, and sexism that prevent people from connecting genuinely. I support The Gathering monetarily and through my physical, mental, and spiritual presence. I work with the video and audio equipment to make sure that the online visitors to The Gathering have an opportunity to see and hear what people who come regularly have an opportunity to be a part of.

The Gathering has been a continuation of many experiences I've had in the past of supporting women and also of redefining myself as a man. I have been redefining myself as a man since I was seventeen years old, and The Gathering is almost like a culmination of that practice. When I was seventeen, I read *The New Man* by Maurice Nicoll and was inspired to look at what men were doing, the incorrect behavior of men in our toxic male culture. It became more important to me to see my reflection in women's eyes. I'd like to believe my narcissistic behavior has been addressed in my development and growth. I spend a lot of time analyzing and thinking about what I do and what I say and how that affects not only myself from within but how it addresses my need to communicate with others. I believe that the reason I draw pictures of people who look like something out of my imagination rather than people I see on a daily basis is that these people represent something other than what I see in myself or in others. Creating a new man has been something I've been thinking about as long as I can remember.

The Gathering has inspired me to look critically at who I am currently as a man, what I am doing, and what makes me come up with my ideas. As a man, I challenge my thoughts that result in my flawed thinking or incorrect behavior. As I continue to redefine myself as a man, I am becoming more of what I am hoping women see as important for men to see. The Gathering has helped me form my identity as a man and as an African. Meeting with these powerful women in discussion about the practice of racism and sexism, I realize that womanists are trying to reach men in a different way, as well as empowering women to be the best that they can be. In The Gathering I am learning about how to redefine myself as a man by putting it into practice. Am I trying to reach out to men differently? Am I trying to be seen by women as other than my toxic male perceived image? My own analysis falls short even though my practice is to empower humanity. The true benefits of being part of The Gathering come from the presence of these womanist preachers and their teaching and interpretations of the Bible.

I hope that The Gathering will one day have a larger congregation and that more people incorporate womanist theology and women preaching into Christianity. Womanist theology and women's preaching will make a difference in church and society by breaking down some of the normative beliefs that men are in charge or men are in control. I hope that will go even further so that we see ourselves as equals rather than opposite sexes and look at ourselves as being more similar rather than different.

Rev. V. Ruth Schulenberg

In late 2018, I started attending The Gathering after pastoring a small congregation in Fort Worth. I had moved to Dallas a few months before and had heard about The Gathering from the Rev. Kamilah Hall Sharp, a PhD student colleague at Brite Divinity School, who had mentioned that she was co-pastoring a new womanist congregation. I wasn't sure whether visiting The Gathering would be an intrusion into what was meant to be a safe space for Black women, or if it was open to all. So, I called Kamilah to find out. She graciously explained that The Gathering was meant to be a place of worship and advocacy for justice amid patriarchy, misogyny, and sexism and to give Black women space for their voices and experiences to be heard from the pulpit. She warmly invited me to attend and since then, I have found that when they say, "all are welcome . . . really," they mean it.

When I arrived for my first worship service there, it turned out to be an end-of-the-year visioning session and dinner to plan The Gathering's ministry goals and intentions for 2019. I was impressed that the discussion focused on social justice issues, particularly full inclusion of people often marginalized by both church and society, and advocacy for positive social change in Dallas and beyond. That was a sharp contrast to similar new-year planning sessions I had witnessed at other congregations where I have pastored or belonged. That is, such planning sessions often focused more on serving the needs and desires of the most active members and regular attenders for meaningful social or educational opportunities (e.g., all-church picnics, fall festivals, Lenten studies, etc.). Instead, at The Gathering, the focus has been on things like advocating for paid leave for often low-paid workers in Dallas and removing statues that honor historical figures who upheld the institution of slavery at the expense, then and now, of the dignity and well-being of our Black community members.

It did not take long for me to decide that I wanted to be a ministry partner of The Gathering or for me to be asked to serve primarily by offering Communion meditations or prayers during worship services. That is, in addition to giving financially to The Gathering and attending regularly in person or via our Facebook livestream, I have been blessed to have many opportunities to share reflections on how justice and celebration of Communion intersect. At first, I thought Rev. Dr. Irie Session, co-pastor with Rev. Hall Sharp, was just being gracious when she would tell me enthusiastically that my Communion meditation had been meaningful to her. I was self-conscious because, as a white woman, I am well aware that I get many opportunities for my voice and my thoughts to be heard, so I want to "pass the mic" as often as possible to others, particularly Black women, who do not experience that privilege. However, at the next annual visioning night, for 2020, Dr. Session and several other people encouraged me to begin writing a book of Communion meditations that could be useful to other congregations who need to see that the Communion table is an invitation into the beloved community.

Rev. Dr. Martin Luther King Jr. wrote in his autobiography: "The aftermath of nonviolence is the creation of the beloved community, so that when the battle is over, a new relationship comes into being between the oppressed and the oppressor . . . The way of acquiescence leads to moral and spiritual suicide. The way of violence leads to bitterness in the survivors and brutality in the destroyers. But the way of nonviolence leads to redemption and the creation of the beloved community."[9] From that perspective, an invitation to Christ's table is an invitation to build a new relationship between those who have been oppressed and those who have been engaged in oppression of others. That starts with some recognition that each of us may simultaneously be in both roles. I can oppress others, consciously or unconsciously, based on my white privilege, while also being oppressed based on my gender in a patriarchal world. So, what does that have to do with Communion? Hours before he would be publicly shamed, tortured, and crucified, Jesus washed his disciples' feet, even the feet of his friends who would betray or deny him and even though he knew that the betrayal and denial were already in the works. Some of us are set to betray and deny our siblings in just a matter of moments or hours, whether through acts of microaggression or greater acts of violence, often while feeling reassured that we are doing our religious duties or being good, decent people. Others

9. King, *Autobiography*, 125, 134.

among us are stinging from the betrayal and denial of people who cluelessly proclaim that we "don't see color," not knowing that such statements imply an inability or unwillingness to see and value neighbors for whom race and color shape their daily experiences of oppression, as well as their sense of belonging to communities of solidarity amid that oppression.

As I sit in the pews or watch the livestream of The Gathering, I live in that tension. It is uncomfortable and it is exactly where I need to be. As Dr. Session said in one of her sermons, "Being anti-racist is taking the risk of sitting with discomfort while listening to another person's truth." I am learning to live with the discomfort of hearing other people speak their truths in ways that provoke me to much-needed change. At The Gathering, my experiences and opinions are challenged and de-centered in a rare context where the experiences, struggles, and joys of Black women are placed up front in the pulpit and at the center of the conversation.

In that setting, how could I not be challenged to join in and call others to "communal repentance," as Dr. Session called it in that same sermon. She was making the point that God wants communal wellness, which means confessing and repenting of the ways we undermine other folks' flourishing. Wellness at individual and communal levels never just happens. It's not a matter of some magical transformation, but a matter of the Spirit calling us to repentance, to the hard work of changing our ways of thinking and being no matter what the cost to our pride, our privilege, and our personal interests.

It also isn't about some vague notion of "white guilt" for me; it's about my redemption and liberation as both oppressed and oppressor. It's about the womanist practice of "Talking Back to the Text" of Scripture, interrogating the ways I have read biblical writings with the lens of my own privilege. As a white feminist, I have been challenged over the years to embrace Black legal scholar and professor Kimberlé Crenshaw's concept of intersectionality[10] to interrogate the ways multiple aspects of identity compound discrimination and disadvantage. I have been slow to see how biblical hermeneutics generally and my own in particular have been shaped by white supremacy, as much as it has been by patriarchal practices I resisted in my high school years way back in the 1980s. I never liked having to mentally reconfigure noninclusive biblical translations to include women and girls, as in the case of the NIV translation of Matthew 4:4: "Man shall not live on bread alone, but on every word that comes from the mouth of

10. Crenshaw, "Mapping the Margins," 1241.

God." (I love bread, so I used to joke that apparently women and girls can, in fact, live on bread alone, since the text only speaks about "man.")

What is not a joking matter is that white supremacy, as much as patriarchy, continues to shape how we translate and interpret Scripture. Further, our hermeneutics shape and are shaped by sometimes toxic theologies. I knew that before coming to The Gathering, of course, but I had never seen that reality named and challenged in each and every sermon in a congregation. As a preacher myself, I have tried to "talk back to the text" (without knowing to call it that) in the past by inviting my congregations to rethink their automatic assumptions about "who" they/we are in the parables or to reexamine interpretations that keep people marginalized. Yet, it is quite a different thing to highlight, week after week, the truth that white supremacy holds the church captive in our hermeneutics, theology, and religious and spiritual practices.

As a personal example, when The Gathering hosted a "Purple Table Talk" about Robin DiAngelo's book *White Fragility: Why It's So Hard for White People to Talk About Racism*, I was reminded of what I would call the dangerous power of white women's tears in derailing discussions of Black women's terror. As a white woman, I may be conscious of the ways female tears have been stigmatized in many places, from the workplace to intimate relationships. I am socially programmed, though, to be unaware of or to deny their power to elicit a violent sympathy from others when they perceive that those tears were provoked by a Black woman's anger. The classic example is a Black woman talking about being the target of racism in the workplace, while a white woman responds by tearfully lamenting that she "didn't mean to cause harm and doesn't have a racist bone in her body." All too often, others will rush to comfort and reassure the crying white woman, while ignoring or even admonishing the Black woman who has just expressed her own very real pain from racism. Regardless of how it is expressed, the Black woman's pain is frequently minimized, dismissed, or even attacked in the face of white fragility about the topic of racism.[11]

So, I am learning to tame my tears, not because of patriarchal stigma, but because I realize they have disproportionate power to draw attention to myself when the attention needs to stay focused on a Black woman's words. This is particularly true in congregational life, where U.S. religious communities still remain racially divided and where predominantly white congregations largely are resistant to addressing the ways racial injustice

11. DiAngelo, *White Fragility*, 133–34.

frames experience of faith and community life. For many women, tears express not just sadness, but anger (for lots of reasons related to socialization against anger). However, my time at The Gathering has taught me that my tears can never be for my sake alone, but should be harnessed so the underlying sadness, anger, and even rage are directed at dismantling systems of oppression from which I gain advantages I have been socialized to ignore. Whether I "feel" power or privilege is irrelevant. Disparate privilege and power are real and must become tools in a collective effort to tear down the hierarchies that reinforce these disparities, keeping us from meeting as children of God, equally beloved and equally valued by our Creator and, finally, by our faith communities.

Diana Clark

I heard about The Gathering by knowing Dr. Session. Twelve years ago, I met Dr. Session when she led a workshop. She wasn't Dr. Session then; she was just Irie Session. I was involved in a nonprofit called Garden of Gethsemane, and she came to help the ministry; we were trying to reach out to women. She came to talk about women in the Bible and women in general. We never know who we're going to meet who are going to be in our lives.

On my journey of faith, I've learned from Dr. Session. At the time I met her she was in a nonprofit; she was always fighting for justice for women and people in general. Then she started New Life Christian Church, and I went to that church. I'd had no desire to attend church, but I began attending church and became active in that church. I was always there. Sometimes in our lives we're just there, just showing up. When she became co-pastor of Rosemont Christian Church, I started attending that church. There I also saw her interact with so many different types of people, and that attracted me because I've always been in the social work field; I was always around people who care about other people. I've been mostly in the helping industry, helping and teaching people, because that's what I saw when I was growing up. My mother was in the helping industry, and a lot of people around me were in the helping industry.

When Dr. Session became the senior pastor of Warren Avenue Christian Church, I went there because I considered her my pastor. She helped me learn about getting involved in church. In my younger years, I attended church. In my teenage years and early adulthood, I wasn't attracted to church, but when I met her I started gradually caring about church, attending church, being involved in church, and learning about church.

I came to The Gathering mainly because of my pastoral relationship with Dr. Session. I've been with The Gathering since day one. I listened to her talk about it, so it was a normal thing for me to be a part of The Gathering. I heard about The Gathering through Dr. Irie and the people around her who were encouraging her to start it, although she didn't want to do it. But she was being a pastor, from my impression. She was talking to people about how Jesus can help them, and she was giving her life as an advocate for other people. She's always wanted to encourage other women, because she knows what it feels like to be a woman in any church. So that's the reason I started at The Gathering. It was just a natural thing. It wasn't anything I had to think about too often. I just said "of course," and I showed up. I wanted to be supportive, and I kept showing up every week. I met Rev. Kamilah Hall Sharp, the other co-pastor, and developed a relationship with her and with everybody at The Gathering. Everybody at The Gathering has a part. It is a gathering, I would say, a gathering of relationships.

I didn't expect The Gathering to be a church. I thought it would just be a place for studying the Bible. I never thought it would be a church, if you think about the traditional church. It was different from most churches. It wasn't my experience of church. The Gathering is different from churches I've been to in that women are pastors. That's the main reason why it started. That's the premise of The Gathering, to hear Black women preach. No men will be preaching there. That will not happen. The Gathering pastors, Dr. Session and Rev. Hall Sharp, preach and teach with more openness to questions. They want people to understand. When I talk to people about The Gathering, some people are not ready for that. They're not ready because their minds have been conditioned and are very hard to change. Unless you're looking for change, it's hard to find it. You have to be looking, searching, open.

The Gathering is a church where all are included. The open table is also really important to me. The Communion table at The Gathering includes everybody. That's very crucial. I'm open to include other people who usually don't get the opportunity to be included. Since I was a very young girl, I wanted to be included. I knew that the worst thing in the world was not being included. I can't say I wasn't included in church, because I attended an African Methodist Episcopal church, so I was always included. But as I became older, I heard my parents talk about being excluded. During segregation we were always together, going to this store and going to that store. When I got older, I had to go out into the world in school and in the work force, and I could see that I wasn't included. It was racial discrimination, not to mention being a woman. Exclusion is something nobody wants.

When I got out there in the world, I experienced prejudice as a woman and as a Black woman. When I became an older adult, I started hearing and realizing what it was, and said, "Oh, OK," and then just recently put a name on it, "sexism." An important part of The Gathering for me is the preaching against sexism and racism, dismantling racism and sexism. I didn't know you could dismantle them, not at all. It was just like eating a piece of apple pie. You have the apples and the sugar and the cinnamon and you have the crust, and you just eat it. How do you change it—no sugar? I couldn't wrap my head around how anything could be changed, but I need to wrap my head around it now. The Gathering has given me hope that we can change things. The Gathering has changed me, inspired me to open my mouth, to show up. Before that I wouldn't open my mouth and say anything, no matter what I felt.

Before I started attending The Gathering, I worked with others to start a nonprofit called Youth Conflict Resolution Center. I was doing mediation, and I was out in the community, and somebody saw me working with children and youth. Other people put the paperwork all together to become a nonprofit. We had meetings and groups to talk about it, and then we named it. I had been showing up, doing different things. The person who was doing all that paperwork died, and I just kept it going. I kept it alive, because I feel like youth really have a voice too. People don't hear them sometimes. People holler at them, but don't get to hear what they really say. People need help to learn conflict resolution, how to get along in their daily lives with the issues that they have. My experience of The Gathering has definitely influenced my work with Youth Conflict Resolution Center. Now I really encourage youth to speak up. I encourage them to do different programs there to help them. I promote the projects at The Gathering to encourage people to support the Youth Conflict Resolution Center.

At The Gathering I've learned how to talk, look, and act in the LGBTQ community. I never really knew how to do that. That's another thing I've learned from The Gathering. Actually what that means is to really see LGBTQ people, to understand that what some teach that the Bible says is absolutely wrong, and to believe that all people ought to be included. I'd been taught by other churches that LGBTQ people shouldn't be included, no doubt about it. And not just churches; the media, the community, nobody talks about it. I was walking around in a daze before, with blinders on, not really knowing what was going on. But The Gathering has helped me to really see. For example, on Martin Luther King Day I was out in the community attending the parade. I walked down the street and I saw a table that had a sign with HIV on it. I asked the woman at the table, "Are you still doing something about HIV? I never hear about it like I used to in the community. I don't hear people talking about it any more. Twenty years ago that's all you would hear in the health community." She said, "Yes, it's still rampant in the community. We're still out there with advocacy." Even though it's illegal to discriminate against LGBTQ people, people still do. It's the same way with discrimination against Black people. I feel the same way about people still using the "n" word; it's illegal, but people still use it. People still do a whole lot of things that are illegal. At The Gathering I've learned to be more aware and open to LGBTQ people.

At The Gathering I've also learned about the word "womanist." I'd never even been taught that. I think "womanist" means working for the good of Black women and everybody. Before The Gathering, I'd heard about womanism in passing, but never really looked at it or acted on it. Now I'm looking at it and acting on it; it has become part of my life. There may be things present in our lives, but we don't really understand them. The Bible is like that too. It may be in our lives, but we don't understand it because we're being misguided. That's why teaching is so important. Another thing I like about The Gathering is that the pastors are teachers. Teaching is critical. I've learned about many women in the Bible I'd never heard of before. I'd heard about women like Mary, Ruth, and Bathsheba, but there are these other women that I didn't know were there. And women like Bathsheba have been taught as evil; it's always one-sided. I was just amazed to learn more than one side about women in the Bible and about other things in the Bible. That's also what draws me to The Gathering.

I became a ministry partner in The Gathering because I'd been showing up all this time. Actually I am becoming a ministry partner, because it's a process for me. I have all the qualifications to be a ministry partner: being consistent in attending worship services, sharing my talents, giving financial support, and actively participating. I'm responsible for preparing the Communion elements each week. Because of the way I was raised, I believe that any type of membership in any organization means I need to be active in it. But "partnership" is a big word. I had to really think about partnership.

What does that really mean? It sounds good and looks good. When I think about a partner, I think about a contract. But I'm just accepting being a ministry partner, and still discovering what it means to be a ministry partner. I'm letting the process work on me. The Gathering is about letting the process work on us. The more we hear, the more we believe. The more we do something, the more it's part of us.

The Gathering is making a big difference in my life. I'm learning so much and meeting so many people. Meeting new people has been really important to me. Seeing how kind people are has made a difference in my life. I'm usually standoffish, keeping to myself. The Gathering is helping me to develop more relationships. People at The Gathering approach me and invite me to take part. I've found my voice. One of the most important things about The Gathering is feeling included and really being included.

At our annual Vision Night meeting, Rev. Kamilah gave a report on the number of people who participated in The Gathering during the past year, including those who joined us online. I looked at the numbers and realized that The Gathering was bigger than I knew. I feel that ten years from now, "Wow!" That's all I can say, "Wow!" I've been here from the beginning, and I want to be in the future of The Gathering.

Olivia Gray

When I had just returned to Dallas after living on the East coast for twenty years, I looked for a church to attend. I heard about The Gathering, and I'm so glad I showed up there. The idea of three Black women ministers leading a congregation was intriguing to me.

When I lived in Maryland and Washington, DC, I was a member of Episcopal churches with women priests. We had gone through the struggle and then acceptance of women and LGBTQ folks as priests. So, when I found out about three Black women preachers leading a congregation in Dallas, Texas, I had to come.

My first time at The Gathering was not long after the beginning of the church. The warm welcome I got from everyone there deeply impressed me. Also, I loved that Communion was served at every service.

But the one thing that really rocked me was this "womanist/womanism" that they talked about. What did they mean? Was this a new woman cult? Where is Jesus in this scenario? I hadn't heard about womanist theology or womanist preachers and didn't understand the significance of the difference their message brought to the table. At first it sounded like they were against male preachers, and this struck a bad chord in me, right into the patriarchal teaching from my fundamentalist evangelical background. Their womanist message uncovered areas that I didn't know existed or didn't want to revisit because of the pain I had experienced, so I recoiled. I was disturbed! I hadn't been challenged with this womanist theology nor had I thought about my evangelical fundamentalist foundation in years. My evangelical fundamentalist tradition had taught me that women couldn't stand in the pulpit and teach men, even when I felt God's call on my life to ministry. Women could stand and teach women all day long. But men were the leaders and teachers and interpreters of the Word, and women were to be supporters only. Even in my uneasiness with all these questions rising up, I kept coming back to The Gathering. Why? Because I was being fed and challenged spiritually to seek and ask questions.

I have grown in my understanding of "womanism." It no longer sounds like a bad word to me. I have been challenged to ask questions and to seek answers about what the Bible really says and what it doesn't say. The Gathering accepts all of who I am: lesbian, Black, woman, child of God, woman loving woman, discerning my call to ministry in a welcoming environment. I feel that the preachers are supportive of my call and are willing to help me in my discernment process.

When I had been at The Gathering for about a year and a half, I decided to join as a ministry partner. I thought my travel commitments were over and I had settled in Dallas at my new home, so I felt a need to become more involved. I started singing as part of the music ministry and took part in the Teresa Fry Brown Conference[12] as the registrar. This past year I also decided to join the altar Communion ministry. I had received so much from The Gathering, and keeping my gifts hidden just didn't seem right. I wanted to be a part of this revolutionary, transformative worship experience that had done so much to expand my Bible study and spirituality.

The Gathering, A Womanist Church has awakened in me an aspect of social justice that I knew about on the periphery, but had never really acted on or gotten involved with. It was always somebody else's problem. If a justice issue didn't affect me personally, then it was somebody else's

12. In 2016, The Gathering co-pastors created the Teresa Fry Brown Women's Preaching and Leadership Institute to empower Black clergywomen and other women in ministry to become transformative leaders. This institute is named for Fry Brown, a minister and preaching professor and director of Black Church Studies at Candler School of Theology at Emory University in Atlanta.

work to do, not mine. Now I know from experience that this attitude could get somebody hurt. For the past year, I have been living very close to losing everything. But God has used people to come through for me in ways that I never expected. I have had to borrow money from friends, and The Gathering paid for my gas for five months so I could get around. I have a roof over my head and a car to get around in, and my electricity is still on, all because of trusting God to show up and asking people to help. I am amazed that I am sharing this now, but I feel it is important to share these blessings of God. I am a very grateful woman! The Gathering reminds me that if I don't ask, then I won't receive.

Now I understand that affordable housing for seniors is a social justice issue. For me, seniors having an affordable place to live is paramount. The Gathering has challenged me to find my voice and use it, to talk about social justice until someone listens.

Another thing The Gathering has done for me is open my eyes to obscure biblical women who accomplished remarkable feats. Dr. Irie Session, one of the co-pastors, led a Bible study on women in the Bible. I learned about many outstanding women leaders I'd never heard about. For example, Sheerah who built three cities: Lower and Upper Beth-horon and Uzzen-sheerah (1 Chronicles 7:20–24). "Uzzen-sheerah" means "listen to Sheerah." Listen to a woman. Listen, because she is a badass woman![13] These cities that she built are still standing in Palestine today.

My vision for the future is that The Gathering will raise up more womanist preachers to spread throughout the Dallas area, then Texas, and beyond. I'd love to see The Gathering multiplied in every suburb in Dallas, Texas, then in every state of the Union, and throughout the world. I envision these womanist churches dismantling patriarchy, misogyny, and sexism (PMS). Churches like The Gathering honor the power and expertise that women bring to the liberation of women and men.

Rev. Dr. Jann Aldredge-Clanton

For many months I had been hearing about The Gathering, A Womanist Church, meeting every Saturday at Central Christian Church in Dallas. Our Dallas Interracial Clergywomen's Group and New Wineskins Community had been talking about visiting this church, and I had connected with The Gathering through worship services online.

13. See Session, *Badass Women of the Bible*, 20–27.

In October of 2018 I heard Rev. Kamilah Hall Sharp, one of the co-pastors of The Gathering, give a presentation at Memphis Theological Seminary's Scholars Week in collaboration with Equity for Women in the Church, an ecumenical organization I co-chair with Rev. Sheila Sholes-Ross. Rev. Hall Sharp gave me new ideas about developing the egalitarian ministries of New Wineskins Community and Equity for Women in the Church. Also, she stirred my thinking about ways New Wineskins Community and Equity for Women in the Church could collaborate with The Gathering, since all three have a mission of dismantling patriarchy, racism, and sexism. Also, Rev. Dr. Irie Lynne Session, the other co-pastor of The Gathering, had recently come on our Equity Board.

With this purpose of collaboration in mind, I first attended The Gathering, A Womanist Church, the Saturday evening after Rev. Hall Sharp's presentation. The Spirit had much more in store for me at The Gathering. What I had not realized was how much I needed The Gathering for my own spiritual healing, empowerment, and growth.

That Saturday evening I went to The Gathering with my friend Rev. Colette Numajiri, one of the co-leaders of New Wineskins Community. Rev. Winner Laws, minister of congregational care and spiritual support, welcomed us and guided us to the sanctuary where Rev. Hall Sharp and Rev. Dr. Session warmly greeted us.

It was evident from the beginning that The Gathering walked the talk of being an egalitarian church, and that this alternative model of a non-hierarchical church works well. The Gathering has "ministry partners," instead of "members," who participate with the co-pastors in worship services, social justice ministry, and administration. The worship service that evening began with Anaya Sharp, eight years old, giving the welcome in a strong, clear voice.

One of the most innovative and fun parts of the worship service was "Greet & Tweet." Many services have a time for people to greet one another and "pass the peace." But this was the first time I had ever experienced a time to greet people, take selfies, and post them on social media. During "Greet & Tweet" I continued to receive the gracious welcome of The Gathering, and was impressed by this creative way to spread the good news about the church.

Holy Communion was open to all. Rev. Hall Sharp welcomed everyone to the table. She and one of the ministry partners served Communion, as everyone in the congregation moved forward to participate. Faith Manning, minister of music, contributed her talents throughout the service, playing meditative piano music during the greeting, call to worship, prayers, and Communion, and between parts of the service. My worship experience continued to expand through this music woven throughout the whole service, instead of at specified times as I was accustomed to in many churches. At The Gathering I have also continued to grow in appreciation of various styles of music, from gospel to jazz to classical.

On this evening Rev. Dr. Session delivered the sermon titled "Deliver Us from the Lies We Believe." It was the first sermon I had ever heard focused entirely on the evil of domestic violence. Before her sermon she prayed for guidance, beginning with "God Our Mother, Father, Creator, Restorer." Rev. Hall Sharp also included "Our Mother" in her prayers. They understand the importance of dismantling the foundation of patriarchy through including female names for God.

Rev. Dr. Session began her sermon stating that "The Gathering doesn't worry about making people mad" by addressing social justice issues, like domestic violence. Quoting Psalm 140:1, "Deliver me . . . from evildoers; protect me from those who are violent," she asked, "What does deliverance look like in a relationship with one person having power over another?" We need deliverance from the lies people believe about Ephesians 5, the "misogynistic interpretations" that give husbands power over wives.

"As a womanist preacher I have concern for all," she proclaimed. "Violence against the vulnerable is not an individual, but a systemic problem. Black women are about three times as likely as white women to die from domestic violence. It is one of the leading causes of death of Black women."

For many years in my feminist writing, I had cited statistics about domestic violence; for example, in the United States alone every nine seconds a woman is battered and one in three women in the world experiences some kind of abuse. But I had not included that Black women are about three times as likely as white women to die from domestic violence. In my white privilege I had overlooked the disproportionate suffering of Black women. At The Gathering I was discovering why I needed womanist as well as feminist perspectives.

Drawing from author bell hooks, Rev. Dr. Session called for using the term "patriarchal violence," instead of "domestic violence," because "domestic" makes the violence seem like an "intimate and private matter, overlooking the roots in male dominance and sexism." This was the first time I had ever heard "domestic violence" called "patriarchal violence," and I agreed this term is more accurate.

The Bible, she said, has been used as a "trap that keeps women in abusive relationships." Survivors of patriarchal violence "believe lies" that come from the misinterpretation of the Bible. "The church is infected with the virus of patriarchal Christianity. Patriarchal Christianity is not the gospel. When Scripture is interpreted to perpetuate patriarchal Christianity, it is not good news. Patriarchal Christianity creates toxic masculinity, which leads to violence. Patriarchal Christianity that leads to patriarchal violence is based on lies. Patriarchal privilege, patriarchal violence, and patriarchal Christianity are evil. They are lies we have believed." She concluded her powerful sermon by challenging us to stop believing lies, to speak out against these lies, to interpret Scripture correctly, to speak the truth that male and female are created as equals in the divine image.

Another innovative part of the worship service, "Talk Back to the Text," followed the sermon. In keeping with womanist practice, "Talk Back to the Text" values every voice, giving everyone an opportunity to engage in conversation about the text and the sermon. That evening several people commented on how refreshing it was to hear a sermon proclaiming the truth about patriarchal violence and patriarchal Christianity. Even though it was my first time at The Gathering, I felt free to comment. I mentioned how much I appreciated naming "patriarchal violence" and connecting it with misinterpretations of the Bible that have resulted in patriarchal Christianity. People in the online congregation also left comments, for example, "We need a collective deliverance . . . *yes*!"

After that first worship experience, I looked forward to participating in The Gathering. In this community I continued to find new insights and new inspiration. I have learned more about how Black women have overcome the triple oppressions of sexism, racism, and classism, and have been inspired and empowered by their stories. Also, from the co-pastors' womanist sermons I have discovered ignored biblical women, such as Sheerah, who built three cities in Israel, and Achsah, who asked for property in a time women were considered property.

Rev. Hall Sharp featured Achsah in a sermon titled "Womanist God-Talk: Ask for What You Want." Pointing out that "Achsah was a pawn in the game of power her father was playing, caught up in a system where other people were making decisions about her life," Rev. Hall Sharp continued: "In the words of Sofia from *The Color Purple*, 'I know what it's like.' You see as a Black woman living in the United States of Amnesia, I find that people seem not to remember that Black women have been crushed by decisions of white supremacy, sexism, and classism since the day they were brought to these shores. I felt that Achsah had some experience, some information, that could help me and all of us."

Drawing from author Audre Lorde, Rev. Hall Sharp proclaimed that oppressed people "in order to survive have always had to become familiar with the language and manners of the oppressor."[14] She challenged us to learn from Achsah, who knew the system wasn't set up for her, a system in which men made all the decisions about her life, and men didn't care about her true value. But Achsah "didn't just watch the game; she figured out how to add another player and how to change the game." Achsah asked for what she needed because she believed in her own worth, even though the unjust patriarchal system she lived in did not value her. "So many times people in the world will try to make us believe we are less than, especially to make people of color, women, and LGBTQ folks believe this. We are created in the image of God, so we're good, we have value. You can't keep waiting for somebody else to ask for what you need or what you want. You have to ask for yourself." As womanists, "we are committed to the survival of all people." Rev. Sharp concluded her inspiring sermon by declaring she had learned from Achsah that in order for everybody to have what we need and not only survive but thrive, we have to ask for what we want.

What I also learned from Rev. Hall Sharp, Rev. Dr. Session, and others at The Gathering was that I needed to hear Black women preachers to help me do the necessary internal work to repent and heal from the sin of systemic racism embedded in me by white supremacist culture. Reading the book *White Fragility*[15] and attending The Gathering's Purple Table Talks panel discussion of this book also helped me with this work of healing. Though my reasons for going to The Gathering at first were to facilitate collaboration with other groups and to do justice work by using my white privilege to support the womanist mission, I soon realized I needed The Gathering for my own healing and growth. As I had long advocated for men to experience feminism and female divine names and images not only to contribute to gender equality and justice, but also for their own healing from sexist culture and for deepening their spiritual experience, now I knew how much I needed womanism and the centering of Black

14. Lorde, "Age, Race, Class, and Sex," para. 2.

15. DiAngelo, *White Fragility*.

women's experience for my healing from racist culture and for deepening my spirituality.

So when the invitation came to become a ministry partner in The Gathering, I responded with a wholehearted "yes"! It is a joy to share my gifts in partnership with others in the liberative, transformative justice ministry of The Gathering. The Spirit has called me to partner in this ministry that addresses the social justice priorities of racial equity, LGBTQIA equality, and dismantling what The Gathering calls "PMS" (patriarchy, misogyny, and sexism). Because this justice ministry is needed now more than ever, I am deeply committed to using my voice, my gifts, my privilege, and my platforms to contribute to fulfilling the mission of The Gathering.

My vision is for The Gathering to continue to spread the good news of welcome and liberation for all, to expand our ministry of justice and equity, and to inspire the birthing of other womanist churches around the country and the world. My big vision for the future is that The Gathering will grow in power to transform church and society.

4

Womanist Sermons

WOMANIST SERMONS ARE A distinctive part of The Gathering: A Womanist Church. Sermons preached at The Gathering incorporate womanist theology and womanist biblical hermeneutics, informed by Black women's experiences of struggle, resistance to oppression, survival, and community building. In their interpretation of preaching texts, Rev. Dr. Irie Lynne Session and Rev. Kamilah Hall Sharp, the co-pastors of The Gathering, draw from their experiences and from the stories of other Black women.

This chapter illustrates womanist preaching with sermons of the co-pastors, delivered at The Gathering.

Growing Forward (Acts 8:26–32)

Rev. Kamilah Hall Sharp

In July of 2017, Rev. Y,[1] Dr. Irie, and I met at a Starbucks to discuss creating a new worship experience here in Dallas. We prayed about it and said we would see where the Spirit leads us. I still am not sure exactly what God is doing, but I know that God is doing something here at The Gathering. And to be honest, I'm in awe of whatever it is that God is doing because every week people show up here. Every week people tune in on Facebook from around the world. And I'm not exaggerating, because in addition to people we know who are watching throughout this country, we have an online

1. Rev. Yvette Blair-Lavallais, former co-pastor of The Gathering, co-founded The Gathering with Rev. Dr. Session and Rev. Hall Sharp.

Gatherer who watches from Ireland. I believe the Spirit is in fact moving and God is definitely doing something in and through The Gathering. As I sat and reflected on The Gathering and the gatherers, this particular text came to mind.

We decided some time ago to preach from the book of Acts for the month of April. Acts has so much going on as we begin to see the early church take form. We see that the followers of the Way are focused on the Spirit, prayer, being inclusive, caring for all in the community. While at the same time living with the tension of what it means to be a community with different people and moving parts. I believe we also see what it can look like when the community starts to grow and expand.

In Acts 8, we have the story of Phillip meeting an Ethiopian eunuch traveling back home. I have heard many preach about the importance of baptism and spreading the good news about Jesus from this passage, and I think these are ways to interpret this passage. I see that and some other things. What does it mean for one of the first expansions of the church to be done through a Black queer worshiper? I know we do not often talk about that part of this passage, but let's look at the text.

"An Ethiopian man was on his way home from Jerusalem, where he had come to worship. He was a eunuch and an official responsible for the entire treasury of Candace" (Acts 8:27 CEB). This is the CEB translation, but y'all know I go to the Greek because sometimes things are translated differently. Some things are lost in translation, and honestly, I just have to read it for myself. So, I went to the Greek and it read that he was Αιθιοψ (*aithiops*), which is translated "Ethiopian" and literally means "scorched face" or "burnt faced." Now we all know when something is scorched or burnt, it is darker and usually Black. When you burn your toast, what color is it? As a Αιθιοψ (*aithiops*), he was a person with Black skin.

And this Black man, the text says, was a eunuch. What we need to understand is that in this context a person could be a eunuch by nature, force, or by choice. Eunuchs did not fit easily in gender identity categories because their gender was considered ambiguous, and as a result they were marginalized by their society. Yet, because they were not viewed as "manly," they were allowed in the private space of women as well as the public space of men. And since they could not have children, we often think that they could not engage in sexual activity, but that is not true. I know you cannot believe I am up here talking about sex in my sermon. I am and we need to do it more often, but not today. My point is the social locations of eunuchs were fluid, and Dr. Pamela Lightsey says, "To identify as queer is to assert a type of fluidity in life, particularly sexually."[2] So, I see the eunuch as queer.

A lot of times we are so busy looking at what is happening that we are not looking at the person it's happening to. But being Black and queer was only part of who he was.

We also know the eunuch was a worshiper because he came to Jerusalem to worship. But he was not just a regular dude; he had some power because he was over the treasury for the queen. So, we have this Black queer worshiping court official who worked for a woman, the Queen or Kandake of Ethiopia. This eunuch was likely extremely educated because he had a scroll to read; people didn't just have a lot of scrolls because they were expensive, and most people could not read in this society. Yet, here he is reading a text written in a language that is likely not in his first language. He is just one of the many examples of educated Black people way back in history, that some folks try to act like didn't exist. This educated Black queer worshiper gives us one of the first examples of talking back to the text. The eunuch is reading, and he has questions.

I love that the Ethiopian eunuch talked back to the text; he had questions and rightfully so. I believe as we grow individually and as a community, we must explore our questions. But I also wonder, what if Philip had let the eunuch ask more questions instead of telling him what it means? Philip told him how he interpreted the text, what it meant to him. I do not believe we allow people space to grow by simply telling them this is what you have to believe. It seems that many times there are people who want to create miniature versions of themselves. They want the people to believe only the way they believe and do only what they want them to do. People cannot grow into who God is calling them to be if we are forcing them to be like us. I'm suggesting that in order for people to grow and for us to grow we have to allow them the space and opportunity to think for themselves about what following Jesus means in their lived experience.

If you received the "Into the Word" email this week, you read more of the passage than I read today and if you haven't read the whole passage, please go back and read it. As the passage continues, Philip tells him the good news about Jesus, and then the Black queer eunuch wants to be baptized. The more I sat with that, the more I realized that this has become the primary way for churches to evangelize and grow their churches. How many times have we been in a church and people are told the good news

2. Lightsey, *Our Lives Matter*, xxi.

about Jesus and then told all you have to do is walk down the aisle and get baptized? I know I have heard it said many times before, but really that's only a partial truth. There is work and some hard days after you walk down the aisle. I believe far too often we fail to tell people what Jesus means in their lives after they've heard the good news, come down the aisle, and gotten baptized. Too often our churches are more concerned about growing the numbers of people in the pews than about helping the people in them grow. In this model, we just tell people about Jesus. It's not enough to tell people about Jesus. What does it mean to follow Jesus? What does it mean to follow a radical Jesus whose intentional disruptions of systematic oppression led to his state-sanctioned execution? So how do we help people to walk and grow in that and what it means?

While I think the model drawn from this passage can be problematic, I also think looking at this passage can help us growing forward. Because one thing I know is that The Gathering does not fit that church model. As Dr. Melva Sampson said on our Womanist Wednesdays broadcast this past week, The Gathering is an innovative disruptor. The design of The Gathering with three women sharing in responsibility and leadership is a disruption to the hierarchal system of traditional church. And she is right. I think if we did not follow that model in our inception, we can't follow that model in our growing forward. So, what does that mean for us?

I believe there are some things that are helpful looking at Philip and the Ethiopian eunuch, and there are some things we might need to do differently. Philip followed the Spirit of God and went to reach out to a marginalized person. I believe that being followers of a radical Jesus calls us to do that as well. "Where all are welcome" cannot just be a slogan; it has to be something we live. I see that one of the first expansions of the church was done though a Black queer body. I believe the passage shows how the church is to be inclusive. For us to be followers of the radical Jesus we must be radically inclusive. When we started The Gathering, we said one of our missional priorities is LGBTQIA equality. We recognized that God has created each and every one of us differently and yet loves us all. And the church should be the place that all God's children can come together. Unfortunately, instead of welcoming all God's children, people have abused and condemned Her children. That cannot be the case here for us. We must make sure this is a space that is safe and welcoming to all, and we must continue to follow the Spirit of God and reach out to people who have been marginalized, pushed aside, and hurt in our society, because that is what this radical Jesus did and that is one way we follow.

Another thing I think we must do differently from Philip in this passage is that we must walk with those who we tell about Jesus or come seeking to learn about and follow this radical Jesus. The eunuch got baptized and never saw Philip again. I understand that the text says the Spirit took Philip away and the eunuch went on rejoicing. I also recognize there are situations where you may not be able to walk with someone for whatever reason. And I believe in our community when we can, we need to stay with people. Don't just tell somebody about Jesus and then don't walk with them on their journey to follow Jesus. In order for us to grow individually and as a community we must walk this journey together, supporting one another and holding each other accountable. People should not have to try to grow on their journey alone. I'm not saying that people cannot grow on this journey alone; I just think growth is better within the community.

OK, those who know me know I'm not really the gardening type. I want to be, but it's just that I have a Black thumb and not because of the melanin in my skin. I'm really bad with trying to keep plants and things alive. It's not for lack of trying or not trying to learn either. I will read and it still does not quite work out with me. But one of the things I read is about companion plants. It's the idea that some plants grow better when they are near other plants than they do alone. This can also be true with food. Native Americans use this idea in their planting with what they call "Three Sisters." They plant corn, beans, and squash together and they grow better because they support each other. The beans provide nitrogen for the corn, the corn provides support for the beans, and the squash becomes a living mulch that suppresses the weeds. Clearly these three items can grow separately, but together they grow even better because of how they support each other as they grow. We are the same way. Yes, we can grow if we walk on this journey by ourselves, but how much better can we grow together? Exploring our questions together? Reaching out to people together? Walking this journey together?

Today is six months since the first worship service at The Gathering. How do we grow forward? We grow forward together as we continue to become what God is calling us into. We grow forward by not separating our faith from what we live, which means we must care about the whole person and our community. We must develop our whole selves as followers of a radical Jesus. This means we tend to our spiritual, physical, emotional, mental, and financial parts of ourselves and those in the community. We must let the Spirit guide us, walk together, and follow this radical Jesus.

Delilah: You Don't Own Me (Judges 16:4–5)

Rev. Dr. Irie Lynne Session

Play song "You Don't Own Me."[3]

"You Don't Own Me" is a song of a woman's resistance to gender stereotypes. It's a woman's song of staking claim to herself as an embodied human being who refuses to be trivialized or trifled with. She sings of taking herself back from any person or ideology that attempts to diminish her right to choose how she wants to live and who she wants to love. She will not be placed in a box of male expectation or fantasy. She does not need male companionship to make her whole, complete, or to feel worthy. Through her lyrics she rejects any kind of treatment deemed harmful to her sense of wholeness. So, she sings loud and self-assured, "You Don't Own Me."

Black Women Owned

The singer characterizes herself as an independent woman with freedom to move about society, self-actualize, and choose from a host of compelling options how to live her life. The woman who sings this remake, Grace Sewell, is white—just like the original singer, Lesley Gore, in 1963. Hearing Kyla Jade, a Black woman who was a contestant on "The Voice," sing the same song, "You Don't Own Me," took on an entirely different meaning for me. When you have the opportunity, listen to Kyla's rendition on YouTube. The difference between the song sung by Grace and Kyla clarifies what is meant when we say, "Womanist is to feminist as purple is to lavender." Same song, different social and cultural ramifications.

Both Women Sing of Ownership

Ownership is lack of independence, mobility, and freedom. We own cars, houses, land, and books. We restrict and approve their use; we own horses, cattle, cats, and dogs; we determine where they live, what and when they eat. These are our possessions—possessions because they are not human beings. We own things. People are not things.

3. Medora and White, "You Don't Own Me."

Women are not things to be owned. Black women are not commodities. However, the way this world is set up—its institutions, systems, and economic structures—it appears Black women are still at risk of being owned. You do know there are ways to own human beings other than physical enslavement?

Here's what I mean. Black women in the United States who work full time, year-round are typically paid just 63 cents for every dollar paid to white, non-Hispanic men.[4] More than four million family households in the United States are headed by Black women[5]—and nearly one in three of those households live below the poverty level.[6] This means that more than 1.3 million family households headed by Black women live in poverty. Contrary to popular and stereotypical beliefs, these disparities are not due to the laziness and lack of drive by Black women. The economic disparity and inequity experienced by Black women is largely due to systemic and structural racism. Yes, there are countless organizations and nonprofits that address the immediate survival needs of Black women and their children. But according to Dr. Keri Day, author of *Unfinished Business: Black Women, the Black Church, and the Struggle to Thrive in America,* such well-intentioned charity does nothing to "address the larger systemic concerns that [cause Black women] to lose confidence in an economic system that exacerbates their cycle of poverty."[7] Which is why I'm excited about the ministry The Gathering is doing with Dallas Black Clergy, a group of Dallas pastors fighting for structural and systemic change in Dallas. Change that will directly impact the lives of Black women and all people who are poor and marginalized. People entitled to a living wage, paid sick leave, affordable housing, and freedom to move around Dallas without reminders of

4. "Current Population Survey," *U.S. Census Bureau* (2017). Unpublished calculation based on the median earnings for all women and men who worked full time, year-round in 2016; full time is defined as 35 hours a week or more.

5. "American Community Survey: Household Type," *U.S. Census Bureau* (2017). Calculation uses family households headed by females living in a household with family and no husband. A family household includes a householder, one or more people living in the same household who are related to the householder, and anyone else living in the same household.

6. "American Community Survey: Selected Population Profile," *U.S. Census Bureau* (2017). To determine whether a household falls below the poverty level, the U.S. Census Bureau considers the income of the householder, size of family, number of related children, and, for one- and two-person families, age of householder. The poverty threshold in 2017 was $19,749 for a single householder and two children under 18.

7. Day, *Unfinished Business*, 31.

white supremacy and the enslavement of African peoples by confederate monuments, honoring those who fought for the enslavement of their ancestors. We reject ownership of Black women and all people. We resist the ownership of ideals, aspirations, hopes, and dreams of entire people.

Our preaching text describes a woman with ideals, aspirations, and dreams, a woman who defied ownership.

Surviving Independently

The book of Judges describes Delilah as an independent, freethinking, single woman, with her own crib and financial resources. There's no mention of parents, a husband, siblings, girlfriends, or an extended family. We don't know her occupation or how she made money to maintain her independence. She appears in Judges as a woman alone. A precarious place for a woman in that ancient time. With no male figures to protect her, she was a woman vulnerable. Yet, somehow, she managed. Somehow each day she put food on her table, paid her taxes, and maintained a home. She managed alone.

Some of us know about making it without a spouse or partner. Some of us know about piecing together an income. We work a little over here, and a little over there, to make rent, pay utilities and car note, and eat. Delilah was an independent woman who pieced together a living for herself in a patriarchal society—where male desire, ideology, preferences, and perspectives were centered and normative. In patriarchal societies the lives of women, children, slaves/servants, and warriors are owned by the patriarchs, whose interests they served.[8]

Because Delilah was a woman with no father or husband to control what she did with her body,

where she took it,
what she thought,
how she reasoned, or
how she made decisions,

and because she was able to provide for herself, Delilah was able to survive to some degree outside the patriarchy. But maybe, just maybe, Delilah wanted more than survival.

Survival is what we do in the meantime. Survival is existing; survival is doing what it takes to not die. I believe Delilah wanted more for herself than to merely exist.

8. Gudorf, *Body, Sex, and Pleasure*, 162–63.

Independent and Dangerous

Dr. Wil Gafney in "Womanist Midrash of Delilah: Don't Hate the Playa Hate the Game" characterizes Delilah as "a true playa for real."[9] With the money she would receive from the five lords, which in today's economy may have exceeded a million dollars—some scholars suggest it could have been as much as a billion dollars—Delilah would've been able to not just survive but thrive. A small price to pay for handing over a man she barely knew, didn't love, and who had been bad news already for two other women and the community. Read the text.

Dr. Gafney describes Delilah as a self-possessed, self-maintained woman who was bad news to patriarchy. Gafney says, "An independent woman with her own resources is dangerous, particularly to patriarchy."[10]

When a woman is in control of her own body and her financial resources, like Delilah, she is presumed dangerous and must be controlled. After all, a woman's body was believed to have the power to "bring down the strongest of men."

Early church fathers, like Tertullian and Augustine, taught the church the dangers of women and our bodies—characterizing us as "the devil's gateway" and "temptress." A woman's body therefore had to be controlled. But no one controlled Delilah's body. Which is why I'm fascinated by Delilah's narrative. When I think of present-day Delilahs, women responsible and in charge of their own bodies and financial resources, I think of Rihanna, Alicia Keys, Pink, Angela Bassett, Oprah, Queen Latifah, India Arie, Gabby Sidibe, and Laverne Cox. But I also think of women of the past: Harriet Tubman, Harriet Baker, Julia Foote, Ella Baker, Sojourner Truth, Madam C. J. Walker, Shirley Chisholm, Ida B. Wells, Jarena Lee, Pauli Murray, and Katherine Johnson.

These women resisted ownership. Some resisted physical ownership and others ideological ownership—understanding that when the mind is free, possibilities are limitless.

Just Ask Jesus

Jesus resisted, refused, and rejected ownership. Perhaps you remember his words, "I lay down my life in order to take it up again. No one takes it from

9. Gafney, "A Womanist Midrash of Delilah," 49.

10. Gafney, "A Womanist Midrash of Delilah," 65.

me, but I lay it down of my own accord. I have power to lay it down, and I have power to take it up again" (John 10:17–18).

Jesus resisted every power and principality designed to own the human mind, body, and spirit. He resisted. Jesus told the powers, "You Don't Own Me."

Say Her Name (Judges 11:30–34)

Rev. Kamilah Hall Sharp

On July 10, 2015, Sandra Bland was traveling in Waller County, Texas, and saw a police officer following behind her so she switched lanes to let him by. DPS Trooper Brian Encinia then pulled her over for changing lanes without signaling. He was initially rather friendly with her, but when he decided he did not like her attitude, things began to change. And when she refuses his request to put out her cigarette, he tells her to get out the car. The following minutes of their encounter are troubling. At one point he threatens to light her up with the taser. At another point she screams; he slams her head on the ground and she says she has epilepsy to which he responds, "good." She is then arrested for supposedly resisting arrest. She ends up in jail on $5,000 bond. Three days later she was found dead in her jail cell. "How did switching lanes with no signal turn into all of this, I don't even know," she says. When the lives of Black girls and women are taken, we are left asking questions like this or trying to figure out why did this happen? But sometimes we don't even hear the story. Sandra's story is one that many of us now know because people spoke up and began to ask what happened to Sandra Bland? So, we know her name. But there are too many women whose lives have been taken, and we don't even know their names.

Which brings us to the passage for today. One that's referred to as "Jephthah's daughter," because we don't know her name and some of us have never heard her story. This particular passage is one that is difficult. Honestly, we can add this to the list of things I said I would never do but ended up doing. When I first read this passage, I said I would never preach this passage. But if we don't, who will? I have been in the church pretty much my entire life. My mother had me in church every Sunday, Wednesdays, and the revivals, and I never heard a sermon on this text. But to be fair, it's not just this text but many texts in the Bible that are never preached, particularly those about women. There are 205 named women in the Bible, not to mention the unnamed women like this one. If we do not bring up these passages and stories, who will?

This passage is so problematic for me. We have Jephthah pushed out of his home by his brothers because he was the outside child born to a prostitute. His brothers decide they do not want to share their inheritance with him because he was beneath them. So, he leaves and later when the brothers find themselves in trouble and the Ammonites are coming for them, they decide to go back and get the brother who knows how to fight.

Jephthah's no fool though; he's not going to fight for these brothers who didn't want him around earlier for nothing. He negotiates what he wants. He tells them that if he fights and wins, then he is the leader and over all of them, and they agree. When he decides he is ready to go to war, he makes this vow to God that whoever comes out of his house to meet him will be offered to God as a burnt sacrifice.

That right there is the problem for me. You see nowhere in the text does it say God asked Jephthah for a burnt offering or for anything. But while dealing with his own insecurities and ambitions, Jephthah made his vow to God and I believe Jephthah did not care that he was most likely offering a woman in his family. You see in this culture when men returned home from war victoriously, women would run out to meet them playing hand drums and dancing. This was how the celebration began. So, when Jephthah was coming home victoriously from war, who did he think was going to come out of the house to meet him?

Jephthah only had one child, his daughter, and she was offered up. How many times have women been offered for sacrifice due to the insecurities or ambitions of a man? Many times, like this daughter, a man she knows and loves. How many times have Black and brown women's lives been offered up for a sacrifice? And let's not forget Jephthah was the leader at this point; he was the one in control. He is part of the governing powers. How many times have those with the governing powers of the state sacrificed the lives of Black and brown women?

But here Jephthah offered to God a sacrifice that God did not ask for. But you know, it's easy for us to be hard on Jephthah, but do we sometimes do the same thing? Do we offer things that God is not asking for? Can we get caught up in our own ambition and insecurities? Sometimes we forget that obedience is better than sacrifice. Let me be clear, Jephthah still does not get a pass. Because you see, the text says when he comes home victoriously, his daughter is the first one who comes out dancing and he immediately starts blaming her. "Oh daughter, you have caused me trouble." Really? She's coming out the house dancing as is the custom, but it's her fault. Victim blaming. Isn't that how it always is? The first thing that happens when a woman is assaulted, raped, and/or murdered is the blame immediately shifts to her. What did she do? Why was she getting smart with the police officer? Why didn't she just be quiet? What was she wearing? Doesn't she have a criminal record? Anything to make it her fault. It's always her fault, let them tell it. Well, I can't let them tell it no more.

Because there are some who suggest that the daughter was willing to be sacrificed. I have even seen some say that she should have protested and maybe even appealed to religious authorities to stop her father. Maybe. But I also have to ask, "Do we always protest when our own bodies are being sacrificed?" Maybe we aren't killed in one instance, but sometimes we are being sacrificed to a slow death that we do not stop. You're looking like you don't know what I'm talking about. Many of you who know me know that I lost my mother to breast cancer in 1999. Yes, cancer was the ultimate cause of death, but my mother did not go to the doctor when she knew she was sick. She was too busy taking care of this person, handling that issue, helping with this, that she continued to slowly sacrifice her own body without protest. I am a firm believer that too many of us do the same. Too often women especially agree to do more and more for everybody at the sacrifice of their own bodies and lives. So, it's hard for me to say, "well, the daughter should have protested," because maybe we should too. "No" is not a four-letter word. You don't have to do everything people ask you to do, especially at the detriment to your life. Sometimes we have to choose ourselves.

The daughter didn't seem to have much choice in this story, but she made one choice we do know and that was to spend her last days with her friends. She asked her father for two months to be with her friends. Biblical scholar Renita Weems says that this woman's story does not end at her death. The story ends with her friends vowing to keep her memory alive and that is the good news. Her death or the one who killed her does not get the last word.[11]

I believe that when our sisters are taken away from us, we cannot allow their deaths to be the end of the story. And we cannot let others hijack the narrative about their life or death. So, they will not make this her fault because we are going to tell her story. We are going to say her name. Her story will not go unheard because we are going to say her name. When

11. Weems, *Just a Sister Away*, Kindle ed., chapter 4.

their version of what happened doesn't seem right, we will speak up, ask questions because we are going to say her name. Her memory will be kept alive because we are going to say her name. We will not forget her because we are going to say her name. We will rejoice in the lives of our sisters and honor them because we are going to say her name.

At this time we are going to call the names of Black women who have been taken from us by state or intimate partner violence. We will call the names of women and ring a bell. When the bell rings, please say, "Say Her Name."

Eleanor Bumpurs
Shelly Frey
Kayla Moore
Miriam Carey

Michelle Cusseaux
Alberta Spruill
Tanisha Anderson
Rekia Boyd

Kyam Livingston
Yvette Smith
Darnisha Harris
Malissa Williams

Shantel Davis
Shereese Francis
Aiyana Stanley-Jones
Tarika Wilson

Kendra James
Sandra Bland
Kindra Chapman
Charleena Lyles

Women taken by intimate partner violence

Karen Smith
Shanna Desmond
Shaquenda Walker

Quanta Nashall Chandler
Shanice Williams
Dr. Sherilyn Gordon-Burroughs
Alicia Trotter

Do You See Us? (Luke 7:36–47)

Rev. Dr. Irie Lynne Session

Several years ago, while I was teaching a class with women leaving the life of dancing in strip clubs and prostitution, Stacey, one of the women in the class, said something I have never forgotten. Interrupting my class, she said to me, "This is the first time I've ever felt seen." Her words pierced my heart. It had never dawned on me what it meant to be seen. I thought certainly she had been seen. Every day and night she caught the gaze of men and women eyeing her body as she danced and glided up and down the stripper pole. Of course, she had been seen. Or had she?

Watched but Not Seen

To see is to perceive with the eyes. It is to recognize and to understand. Stacey had not been seen. She had not been understood; she had only been viewed as a commodity and not as a woman with strengths and gifts that could glorify God and transform the world. What she had been was watched. There is a difference between being watched and being seen. The woman in our text had been watched. To watch is to observe, to view, and to stare at. It typically doesn't involve acquiring knowledge of the object we are watching. People watch our Facebook, Instagram, and Twitter posts. When some of us go to high-end stores like Neiman Marcus or Bergdorf Goodman or Tiffany's, we are watched. When we're watched, our imaginations conjure up scenarios about who a person is and is not. When we watch, we stereotype; when we watch, we misjudge; when we watch, we misrepresent one another.

Watching Is Dangerous

Watching can be dangerous. I believe Jesus understood this. When we watch, we can only make assumptions based on limited and/or false information. Watching activates implicit bias because there is little or no information about who or what we're watching. All we have to go on is what we've heard about who or what we're watching. We have no firsthand experiential knowledge.

All people seemed to know about the woman in the text was that she was a certain kind of woman, a sinner. The text doesn't say what her sins were. It doesn't give any specifics. Perhaps because no one knew. No one took the time to have a conversation with this woman. But they watched her. Watching is dangerous for the one being watched.

Women are watched and raped. Transgender persons are watched and brutalized. Sandra Bland was watched as she failed to signal a lane change. Tamir Rice was watched as he played in the park with a toy gun. Philando Castile was watched as he reached into his pocket to retrieve his ID. Alton Sterling was watched as he sold CDs outside of a supermarket. Sean Bell was watched as he sat in his car before his bachelor party. Renisha McBride was watched while calling for help after an accident. All of these precious human beings were watched and not seen.

Jesus calls out the Pharisee, Simon the Leper, who had probably become one of Jesus' followers after being healed of leprosy. Jesus calls him out for watching rather than seeing.

Religious and Blind

It is possible to be religious and still not see. We can go to church, pray, and read our Bibles and be blind. Just this week I read a post that asked, "Can you be an Elder in the church on Sunday and a racist the rest of the week?" I'll add this, "Can you be an Elder on Sunday and a misogynist the rest of the week? Can you be a movie star with a top-rated show where you have an adopted Black child and be a racist in real life." Yes, you can. It's easy when we're blind and unable to see.

This text makes it clear that one can even be a follower of Jesus Christ and blind. Simon, one of Jesus' disciples, was blind to this woman's true identity and worth. He does not see her as someone who is intrinsically the same as him—worthy of dining with Jesus. No, she was a woman and a sinner; therefore, she was beneath him. She was less than. She was not deserving of a place at the dinner table. Simon's failure to SEE her impacted the opportunities made available to her. We give the benefit of the doubt to those we see. Second chances are for people we see. Big churches are given to people we SEE. Just because someone is religious doesn't mean they see.

Intentional Blindness

Then there are people who don't want their eyes opened. There are people who don't want to see, especially not to the plight of the racially oppressed. Some people are afflicted with intentional blindness. Some people only want to see certain kinds of oppressed people. We'll see the sex-trafficked child in Asia, but not the slick talking fifteen-year-old Black girl in the hood who, after being raped most of her life, shoots the next man who tries to rape her. Our seeing is selective. And I get it. Seeing is painful and uncomfortable. But women like the one in our text, and women like Stacey, need us to see them. Because life has kicked their behinds, they can't see themselves as worthy of respect and dignity. And so, they need to see themselves through our eyes until they can see themselves correctly. Our seeing helps them see. Therefore, we must reject intentional blindness.

God Sees

The good news in this text is that Jesus does see the woman. Jesus sees her clearly. Jesus sees how the community has marginalized her; Jesus sees how she's been misrepresented; Jesus sees her heart and her desire to be close to him; Jesus sees her need for advocacy and he provides it. The good news in this text is that because Jesus sees her, the playing field is level. Jesus exposed her faith and Simon's lack of faith. Jesus amplified her hospitality and confronts Simon's lack of hospitality. Jesus publicly elevated this woman with the bad reputation. Jesus' response to Peter let this woman know, "I See You." Not only did Jesus see this woman, but God sees us. In the Bible we read, "For [God's] eyes are upon the ways of mortals, and [God] sees all [our] steps" (Job 34:21). God sees us. The Bible says, "For the eyes of [God] range throughout the entire earth, to strengthen those whose heart is true to [God]" (2 Chronicles 16:9). God sees us. And because God Sees Us, may we learn to see one another.

The Gathering, A Womanist Church

If It Wasn't for the Women (Luke 8:1–3)

Rev. Kamilah Hall Sharp

It is 2018, and it is January and we are all well aware that this is the birthday month of Martin Luther King Jr. This year marks fifty years since his tragic murder in 1968 in Memphis, Tennessee. Festivities have already begun, and there will be all types of activities and services remembering him and the work he did and rightfully so; he did some significant things and made numerous sacrifices. And what I also know is that Martin and others whose names we know could not have done the things they did if not for the work of many others.

Particularly, if it wasn't for the women, the Civil Rights Movement as we know it would not and could not have been. It's not just the Civil Rights Movement, but so many other things. James Brown told us it's a man's world, but it wouldn't be a thing without a woman or girl. That's true, because the world as we know it would not be possible if it wasn't for the women. And far too often, these are the names we never hear. People don't know what they did, people don't know whom they've helped, and we aren't aware of the ways they have paved for so many after them. We cannot continue to allow their work to go unknown. One such woman is Pauli Murray.

Anna Pauline Murray was a poet, writer, lawyer, activist, and the first Black woman to be ordained as an Episcopal priest. She was raised by an aunt and grandparents in North Carolina after the death of her mother and murder of her father. Her aunt always emphasized to her that she must be the "best of the race." And that is exactly what she continued to strive to be.

Working her way through college at Hunter College, she had to quit for a period after the stock market crashed because she did not have even enough money to feed herself. But she pressed on and worked hard because she knew she had to be the best of the race. While at Hunter she stopped calling herself "Pauline" and started using "Pauli," a more gender-neutral name.

Pauli Murray became active in the Civil Rights Movement early. She applied to attend the University of North Carolina for graduate school, but received a letter stating people of her race were not admitted to that university. Never mind that she had white relatives who attended there, had been on the board of trustees, and had even created a scholarship for students there. She was Black and therefore, unacceptable. She wrote President Franklin Roosevelt and Eleanor Roosevelt to inform them of the injustice she was experiencing, which was the beginning of a life-long relationship with Eleanor Roosevelt. Pauli Murray's pushing the issue paved the way for Floyd McKissick to become the first Black person accepted to UNC Law School. But before Floyd could go to UNC, there had to be Pauli Murray. If it wasn't for the women.

This is not the only area you find Pauli Murray ahead of the class. After seeing injustice after injustice, Pauli Murray decided to go to law school. She was one of the three females at Howard Law School. It was here that she and other students staged sit-ins at restaurants in DC in the 1940s. The forties, twenty years before sit-ins were used by activists in the sixties. But at her time at Howard Law School, Pauli Murray realized that not only was she discriminated against because of her race, but also because of her gender.

At Howard there were opportunities given to the male students that were not offered to the female students. When she graduated at top of her class, she was awarded the Rosenwald Fellowship that should have allowed her to attend Harvard, but Harvard would not accept women in the law school. She wrote a letter to Harvard and said she would gladly change her sex to meet their requirement but was not aware of a way to do that. These experiences made Pauli Murray very much familiar with what she called Jane Crow, but that did not stop her.

Pauli Murray went on to write on equal opportunity in employment. Thurgood Marshall called her book *States' Laws on Race and Color* the Bible for civil rights attorneys. It was her writings that were used to make arguments in *Brown v. Board of Education*. It was her argument that Ruth Bader Ginsburg used to argue at the Supreme Court that the Equal Protection Clause pertains to women. Pauli Murray used her gifts in pursuing what she knew to be right.

While working with others in the movement, such as Ella Baker, Martin Luther King Jr., and Bayard Rustin, she noticed how Black women were doing the work but not allowed in leadership roles and were not part of the national policy-making decisions. The women could do the work but could not lead, and that was a problem. It's still a problem.

Yet long before Kimberlé Crenshaw coined the term "intersectionality," Pauli Murray made it clear that she could not separate her Black self from her female self, from her worker self. She saw herself as a Black female worker in the all but United States, trying to survive. And like so many others, she had struggles. She struggled with her multiracial identity. She struggled with her identity as a woman who loved other women sexually.

Faced with respectability politics, the pressures of her family to be the best of the race, and a sexist society, she never spoke publicly about her sex life. She did not call herself homosexual or lesbian. Pauli Murray experienced emotional and physical breakdowns which caused her to be hospitalized numerous times as she wrestled with how she felt on the inside versus what the world was telling her. She tried to make sense of her life. Pauli Murray believed she was a male trapped inside a female body. This was the only way she could rationalize her feelings for women and her desire to do jobs typically associated with men.

She did not have the language of transgender available to her, and I do not know if that is how she would identify herself. I know she did love other women sexually, which is more accepted today than back then. There are more preachers now, like all of us here at The Gathering, who do not condemn people for living the way God created them and loving who they love. But there still are not enough of them.

I know that Pauli Murray lived in a world where people were persecuted for being same-gender loving even when they were major contributors. Look at how Bayard Rustin was treated. I believe she dealt with her situation the best way she knew how, trying to be the best of the race, all while doing the work necessary to make things better for all people. She did the work and did not get the recognition she deserved. Much like the women in Luke who travelled with Jesus doing the work.

In Luke 8 we are told that traveling through the cities and villages with Jesus and the twelve were some women. The author names Mary Magdalene, Joanna, Susanna, and many others. Y'all know me, when I read this, I had questions. There were many others? Were there so many women with Jesus that you can't name them all? It's always interesting to me that when people discuss these women, they tend to focus on the demons or what they were cured from. Folks like to focus on other folks' past instead of the work. I'm not concerned about the demons or infirmities they had, because the passage states they were cured of that. I want to know about how they walked and worked with Jesus.

But here's the thing: the Greek says that the women *diakoneo* to Jesus and the twelve. The NRSV translates it as "provided"; other translations say "ministered" or "served them out of their resources." I personally translate it as "ministered to them," but even with that, some say they did "women's work" like shopping, cooking, taking care of things for them out of their own money. Others say it was more ministerial work such as preaching and serving like the twelve. Whichever way you want to interpret it, one thing is clear; these women were doing the work. And they do not get the acknowledgments or titles that the men get. You see, Luke tells us the women were there, although he only names a few; he never calls them apostles or disciples although they walked with Jesus and worked with Jesus just like the twelve.

So, their hard work gets overlooked. Their contributions are overlooked. Their names are not well known. Just like Pauli Murray. The women who walked with Jesus and Pauli Murray are all women of action. They not only hear the word of God; they act on it. These women understand that they are the hands and feet of Jesus. These women do things that go unnoticed but make a difference.

The work Mary Magdalene, Joanna, Susanna, and the many other women who walked with Jesus and brought their pocketbooks made it possible for Jesus to travel through cities and towns, healing the sick, raising the dead, and giving people a new life. If it wasn't for the women. The work of Pauli Murray along with many others, some of whom we know their names, many whom we do not, paved the way for us all. If it wasn't for the women.

I believe as a woman who is called by God to preach that I stand here on the shoulders of Mary Magdalene, Joanna, Susanna, and Pauli Murray. I know the work of these women changed the world. We all stand on their shoulders because they made a way for us all. We must acknowledge them and their work. I believe that we honor them by doing what we can to make this world a better place as well. We may not have money like the women with Jesus or preach like them. Maybe we can't write a legal argument like Pauli Murray, but we can do something.

When I look at the women in the passage and Pauli Murray, what I notice is none of them tried to do everything; none of them tried to do it alone. The women with Jesus put their coins together; they ministered together. Pauli Murray worked with Ella Baker, King, Eleanor Roosevelt, and many others to make an impact. Their work together made an impact. All of these women knew they were walking with God, in their God-given authority, using their God-given talents. This is how they made a difference for us all. How can we make a difference if we walk with God, in our God-given authority, and use the talents and resources God has given us?

Racism Is Sin (James 2:1–9 NLT)

Rev. Dr. Irie Lynne Session

I begin this sermon with a quote from Audre Lorde about truth telling, "What's the worst that could happen to me if I tell this truth? Unlike women in other countries, [my] breaking silence is unlikely to have [me] jailed, 'disappeared' or run off the road at night. [My] speaking out will irritate some people, get [me] called bitchy or hypersensitive and disrupt some dinner parties. And then [my] speaking out will permit other women and [men] to speak, until laws are changed, and lives are saved and the world is altered forever."[12] The truth is, people would rather us not speak our truth about racism. They would rather we keep silent. Ignore it. Act as if we live in a post-racial society. But the truth is, we do not. Racism is alive and active. Therefore, I must tell this truth. Here and now.

Pray with me. May we have eyes to see and ears to hear what the Spirit is saying to the church. Amen.

Favoritism and Partiality

In this preaching passage, the Apostle James questions one's ability to have faith in Jesus Christ and simultaneously favor certain individuals or groups over others. The apostle calls the recipients of his letter "brothers and sisters." He writes to church folk. Even church folk favor some people over others.

In the Greek, the word "favor" is actually "favoritism, partiality." It means to have respect of persons, "to lift up the face." To focus on the face of an individual, their appearance, how one looks to be and what one does or does not possess. In other words, in this context "favoritism" is based on external factors—what can be seen, such as wealth, social status, race, gender, and material goods. What James is actually describing here is what's called a "dominance hierarchy."

Dominance Hierarchy

George Lakoff, in his book *Moral Politics: How Liberals and Conservatives Think,* describes the dominance hierarchy this way: "The Rich over the

12. Lorde, "Your Silences," para. 2.

Poor . . . Our Country over Other Countries . . . Men over Women; Whites over Non-Whites; Straights over Gays; Christians over Non-Christians. In each case, the hierarchy limits the freedom of those lower on the hierarchy by legitimating the power of those higher on the hierarchy."[13] Lakoff writes, "In the conservative hierarchy, which explains all Republican policy, certain people are considered superior to others."[14]

The Apostle James calls such ways of categorizing people "discrimination," and declares it the result of evil motives. Think about it. What motivations are lurking just beneath the surface of an individual or racial group's psyche to maintain a dominance hierarchy where they hold the top spot? Greed, arrogance, political power? Whatever the reason, the apostle calls it out as evil!

He makes a compelling case that faith in Christ is antithetical to a dominance hierarchy. Why? Because the apostle understood that a dominance hierarchy means injustice for those on the bottom. Such is still the case today.

A dominance hierarchy does not lead to Christlikeness. When we as a society elevate the ideas, perspectives, race, gender, culture, and experiences of one group over others, we do not reflect the God of justice nor do we honor the Christ who came to love and liberate all people. This evening I'm here to make it crystal clear that showing favoritism and partiality is the essence of racism.

Racism is Partiality

Thomas Jefferson, the third president of these yet to be United States of America, favored the ideas, behaviors, social mores, and capitalist economic systems set forth by whites over those of African and Indigenous peoples. He was partial to and elevated white life, white brilliance, white ingenuity, and white supremacist capitalist patriarchy over Black life. In order to justify the abduction, enslavement, and colonization of African and Indigenous peoples, Jefferson turned to scientists. He suggested there were "natural differences" between the races and asked scientists to find those differences. But his scientific project began with the wrong question. These scientists didn't ask, "Are Blacks inferior to whites?" Instead, they asked,

13. Lakoff, *Moral Politics*, 431.

14. Lakoff, "twitter.com@GeorgeLakoff," https://twitter.com/georgelakoff/status/985951056378060800.

"Why are Blacks inferior to whites?"[15] "If science could prove that Black people were naturally and inherently inferior, there would be no contradiction between America's professed ideals and its actual practices."[16] America could live conscious free with the brutal, vicious, and inhuman treatment of African peoples by whites.

But, how many of you know that when you start with the wrong question, you will always end up with the wrong answer? The question isn't "Why are Black women angry?" It's "What do Black women have to be angry about?"

The question ought not be "Why do women stay in abusive relationships?" but "Why do men devalue and abuse women?" The question isn't "Why are Black and brown people disproportionately shot and killed by police?" but rather "What are we doing about the implicit racial bias of police officers that causes them to fear, shoot, and kill Black and brown people and arrest white people?" When we ask the wrong questions, we'll end up with the wrong answers. The wrong answers are death-dealing for Black and brown bodies. Jefferson began with the wrong question, and the answers to his question embedded racism into the DNA of America.

Racism Is Not

I want to be clear tonight; racism is not merely the dislike of persons of another race. Racism is not white women clutching their purses when a Black man gets on the elevator. Racism is not laughing at racial jokes. Racism isn't conscious hate. Racism isn't believing you're better than another person. Racism isn't prejudice. That's where many of us get it twisted. We all have prejudice. We all make judgments about people before ever getting to know them personally. It's not right, but it's not racism. But, "when a racial group's collective prejudice is backed by the power of legal authority and institutional control, it is transformed into racism."[17]

In other words, my white colleague's implicit bias toward me as a Black woman has no power to affect my life or livelihood unless she shares her misguided thoughts about me with her white supervisor who has the same racial biases and the power to demote, fire, or otherwise impact my career advancement and livelihood. When implicit bias, discrimination,

15. DiAngelo, *White Fragility*, 16.
16. DiAngelo, *White Fragility*, 16.
17. DiAngelo, *White Fragility*, 20.

and prejudice are institutionalized, they become racism. Racism isn't dislike for someone.

Racism is racial prejudice plus the social and institutional power to dominate, exclude, discriminate against, or abuse certain groups of people based on race.

Ask Questions

So, what can we do? How do we make racial equity a reality? Well, the Apostle James gives us at least one solution. The apostle approached the behavior of those showing partiality with a hermeneutic of suspicion. What do you mean, Pastor? Here it is: James questioned the behavior, actions, and attitudes of those professing faith in Christ and discriminating against others based on a dominance hierarchy.

Check out his questions:

1. First, *he questioned their hypocrisy.* How can you claim to have faith in Jesus Christ *if* you favor some people over others? But, he didn't stop there.
2. Then, *he questioned their knowledge of God.* Hasn't God chosen the poor in this world to be rich in faith? You must really not know God if you don't know that!
3. Finally, James *questioned their spiritual insight, their ability to see life as it really was.* Isn't it the rich who oppress you and drag you into court? Aren't they the ones who slander Jesus Christ, whose noble name you bear?

James was masterful!

Asking questions is a beautiful and brilliant rhetorical and therapeutic strategy because it causes people to think about their behavior and actions and then make their own conclusions. And if their motives are pure, they will arrive at a righteous answer. But if they are people who only want to know what they already know, if they are not teachable, if they are arrogant, they'll miss it every time.

Church, what would happen if we just begin asking the right questions? Doing so can be a strategy for ending racism one conversation at a time.

Now, let me be clear; I am not suggesting that Black people are the ones to ask these questions of white people. White folk are the ones who need to ask piercing and thought-provoking questions to their family, friends, and co-workers. I am not confused about this. I have learned a costly lesson as a Black woman that "bringing racism to white people's attention is often seen as not nice and being perceived as not nice triggers white fragility."[18] It is not the responsibility of Black people to end racism. Robin DiAngelo, a white woman and author of *White Fragility: Why It's So Hard for White People to Talk About Racism*, contends, "It is white people's responsibility to be less fragile; people of color don't need to twist [ourselves] into knots trying to navigate"[19] white people's fragility and fear.

White People's Faith

Can I keep it real right in here? Sometimes I want to ask white Christians, "Where is your faith?" Because frankly, I'm sick and tired of hearing them talk about how afraid they are of "asking the wrong question" or "saying the wrong thing," which means they do and say nothing to address racism. Sometimes I just want to scream to the top of my lungs, "Stop being cowards! You say you are followers of Christ; where is your faith in the Christ you say you follow?" Didn't Christ say, "Whatever you ask for in prayer with faith, you will receive" (Matthew 21:22)? Perhaps my white brothers and sisters who are afraid to enter into conversations about racism, or read books about racism, or challenge family and friends on their racial bias, need to pray for courage. Jesus said he would give it to them.

How long are *whyppipo* (white people) going to allow fear to keep them from doing their part in eliminating this social and institutional evil that has infected the church and society? I suggest: activate your faith and start posing questions to your friends and family.

The Apostle James ends his questioning with a call to love. He writes, "Love your neighbor as yourself" (James 2:8). What of this love? And what does love have to do with eliminating racism? Dr. Cornel West argues, "Justice is what love looks like in public."[20] Justice is intricately woven into the fabric of love. One cannot love without a concern for doing justice. Dr. King says, "Justice is love correcting that which revolts against love."[21] Racism is antithetical to love. But some of us are afraid of this kind of

18. DiAngelo, *White Fragility*, 153.

19. DiAngelo, *White Fragility*, 152.

20. West, "Justice is Love Made Public," para. 2.

21. King, "Let MLK Trouble Your Conscience," para. 30.

love—a love that acts in the service of justice for all human beings. If that is your truth, if you are afraid to love like this, let me remind you that God did not give you a spirit of fear or cowardice, but rather "a spirit of power and of love'" (2 Timothy 1:7). The question is, will you believe it? Will you act on that truth? Because the truth is:

- Love can dismantle racism.
- Love speaks when fear would keep us silent.
- Love motivates us to right action when fear summons us to recoil.
- Love tells the truth when fear provokes dishonest dealings.
- Love pushes us past fear of saying the wrong thing and drives us to read and learn in order that we might have informed conversations on racism.
- Love is active participation in transforming church and society; fear maintains the status quo.
- Love strengthens us to sit with our discomfort so we can hear the stories of those we fear.

Beloved, racism, and all its manifestations, is sin. But, courageous love, bold love, love expressing itself in truth telling and right action will dismantle the principalities and powers of racism. Why is this kind of love so important? Because it's the love that Jesus demonstrated. It's the love that kept Jesus on mission. This is the kind of love that Jesus died to make real for us. This is the only kind of love that matters to God. And as children of God it's this kind of love that ought to matter to us.

It's Complicated (Luke 10:25–37)

Rev. Kamilah Hall Sharp

Today we continue the sermon series on food justice where Rev. Y posed the question to us, "When will there be a harvest?" See, food is a necessity of life. We need food in order to survive and to thrive. Yet, each night there are a lot of children and adults who go to sleep with only stomach pains because they didn't have anything to eat. Many children wake up each morning and head to school hungry and/or malnourished, and because their stomach is speaking so loudly, they cannot concentrate on what the teacher is teaching. So, they are often accused of not paying attention or being disruptive, when truthfully they are just hungry.

Hunger pains come in the bodies of so many across the world. People are hungry and for many reasons. As Rev. Y and Dr. Irie told us, people are hungry because of greed, and some systems give a lot to some and little to nothing to others. People are hungry because of policies that give corporations tax breaks while trying to cut SNAP food benefits for people. There are several contributing factors to the harsh reality that many people do not get the food they need, and sometimes it seems so simple, but really it's complicated, much like today's biblical passage.

Today we look at the oh-so-familiar parable of the Samaritan who helps a man in need. I have to be honest; it wasn't until more recently that I began to really appreciate the parables. I used to be like, "Jesus, why can't you just tell them straight up? Enough with the stories." But now I get it. The reality is sometimes folks can't handle the truth straight up; they don't hear you when it's not what they want to hear. And sometimes people remember stories better. I know my memory is a little shady these days; you can tell me your name and I may or may not remember, but if you tell me part of your story I usually don't forget that.

The good thing about the parable, though, is you cannot reduce it to only one meaning. I know people try, but really parables can have more than one meaning, as most things. I know we have heard this text preached so many times, but I want to take a close look at it today and see what it might mean for us who say we are followers of Jesus in this moment.

The passage begins with a lawyer standing up to try Jesus. We've all been there before, right? Folks want to make themselves look good, so they decide to try you. Well, you see Jesus had time on this day. The text says he stood up to test Jesus, and asks Jesus, "What must I do to inherit eternal life?" (Luke 10:25). The funny thing about this is the tense of the word "do" here in Greek is something he just needs to do one time. You know like do x-y-z, check, I got eternal life. I'm good.

But Jesus comes back and asks him, "What does the law say, lawyer? What did you read there?" We often read over that as a simple question because we think of it in our modern times, when most people can read and have access to things to read, but that isn't the case here. We have to remember that most people in this culture were illiterate and extremely poor, and the people who heard Jesus tell this parable were poor or struggling working class people and most of them in danger of starving. To be able to read the law for yourself means you have to have some privilege and means. The lawyer takes two well-known Jewish verses, Deuteronomy 6:5 and Leviticus 19:18, and uses them to answer Jesus question: "love God with all your heart, and with all your soul, and with all your strength, and with all your mind; and your neighbor as yourself" (Luke 10:27).

Jesus tells him, "ding, ding, ding, you got the right answer; now "do this and you will live" (Luke 10:28). Now when Jesus says "do," it is a different tense; it's a different kind of "do." It's an imperative "do"; it's a command and something you might have to do over and over. But the lawyer wants to really show out and he asks, "Who is my neighbor?" (Luke 10:29). That is a very good question, especially in these divisive times we live in. Who is my neighbor?

This is the part of the sermon where we might hear that we need to think more about who is our neighbor. Like the people who are not getting food every day, people experiencing homelessness, the marginalized—these are all our neighbors. Or we could talk about how we live in a global society, and the reality is that just as the man next door whose name we don't know is a neighbor we should be concerned about, so is the Palestinian woman living in Israel under attack. Often we talk about extending our idea of who our neighbor is, and as I sat with this passage I wrestled with this question. I believe both of those are correct, and we need to think even more about who is our neighbor.

But I kept thinking about this and reading; then I remembered Rev. Y preaching a couple weeks ago from Genesis about God creating humankind and the earth, and it was good. God created humankind and the earth, and it was good. What if we considered all of God's creations our neighbor? Meaning all living creatures including the planet on which we live? How could that change the way we interact with the planet that God also created? The hard truth is how we treat this planet that God created matters. How we have treated this planet that God created matters.

This week alone we have not one, two, but three hurricanes approaching. We have much warmer winters, excessive rain that causes flooding, excessive heat that causes droughts, and this means that some people don't get the food they need. When there is flooding and droughts in California, Wisconsin, and so many other places, crops are ruined. Food that we need is no longer available, sometimes creating shortages and higher prices. Which means some people who may have wanted to buy certain fruits and vegetables can no longer afford them because now they are too expensive.

Then we have changes in the ocean temperature that cause calcification in the ocean that kills a lot of animals. Yet there are one billion people depending on food from the ocean as their main source of protein. But these animals are dying or being overfished. So many people do not get the food they need.

Food insecurity is caused by many factors, and it's complicated because so many of the reasons we may not have direct effect on, like policies, poverty, wars, and the economy and then there are some we do. Some of the reasons of food insecurity are because of us.

Oh, I can hear you, wait what? Kamilah, how am I a reason for hunger? I am not keeping food from people. Oh, we all are. How? I will give you two ways, first waste. We waste so much food each day. Let me restate that. I waste so much food every day, and knowing how many children, women, and men do not eat, my waste is not only shameful, but it is sinful. I stand before you today and confess. I'm told confession is good for the soul but bad for the reputation. But I must be honest. The way I waste food is sinful, and I must do better than I'm doing right now.

Another way that we are responsible for hunger is one that we do not think about, and some do not even like to mention, climate change. I know that there are many people who will deny the reality of climate change. I know that the current resident of the White House removed the words "climate change" from all the White House and State Department websites when he took office. But not saying it or ignoring it does not mean that it is not real.

Climate change is when the earth temperature increases each year because of human activity. Yes, humans like you and me. There are things that we do that cause the climate to change. Increased consumption of natural resources and increased emission of greenhouse gases cause climate change. See, we have bought into the idea that more is better. So now it is difficult for us to understand words like "restraint," "sharing," "limits," and "boundaries" because so much of our political and personal lives focus on words like "expansion," "growth," and "development." The reality is the growth model we have built up economically and ecologically is not sustainable. We do not have enough resources to continue at the rate we are going, and Mother Nature does not do bailouts.

We know that this planet is part of God's creation, yet we don't care for it like it is. I know this girl who used to say all the time, "It's all about me." She really believed that; she still does and truthfully most of us do. We have operated in the "me" and "mine" paradigm for so long we forget about "God's." We have no problem trashing God's creation because it's not mine. If you come to my house and I give you a bottle of water and you throw it on my floor and walk away when you finished, we would have a problem, right? Let me tell you we would have a problem. Yet, so many of us have no problem throwing our trash out the window or on the ground because we don't think that caring for something outside of what is ours is our responsibility. We deny that loving God means loving all of God's creation and caring for it because it's inconvenient. Or we sometimes fall victim to moral paralysis; we know what is right, but we do not move to do anything.

We like to say, "Jesus paid it all." Jesus paying with his life does not mean we do not have work to do. When I went to college at the wonderful Florida A&M University, I had a small scholarship and the rest of my tuition my mother paid in full, with her hard-earned money. But my mother's paying my balance did not mean that I didn't have to do anything else to get the degree. I still had to do my part. I had to get up, I had to go to class, I had to study, and I had to pass my exams. My mother's paying the debt only opened the door to the opportunity. Jesus' death and resurrection give us opportunity; it does not take away our responsibility.

Look at what Jesus shows us in his parable; the Samaritan gives of his time and resources to help the person in need. This seems like a situation of death until the Samaritan does something about it. The problems of our planet seem like a situation of death unless something is done. Now we can look at this parable a couple different ways. First, obviously we can look at the work the Samaritan is doing to help. This man is interrupting his plans, using his time and resources to help in a needed situation, and likely did not get anything in return. We can say we need to be like the Samaritan and go do what is right for all of God's creation.

Or we can say what if we are not the Samaritan but the person in need and we are being called to receive help from God, but we can't receive God's help because it's too much stuff keeping us from seeing we need help. We see our beautiful SUVs, but we don't see the harm they're doing to the environment. We see our bags of groceries we bring home, but we don't see the landfills the bags fill up because they aren't recyclable. We see our fresh produce, but not the blood that was shed when the people picked the produce from the soil and cut their hands to get it to us when many of them can't afford to buy any for themselves. There is a cost to everything and not just the price we pay for it. Maybe we have too much stuff and it is keeping us from seeing we need God's help.

I don't know how you will see yourself in this parable, as the Samaritan or the person in need. What is clear to me, though, is however we see ourselves, we have to do some things differently. We must change the way we think so that we can change our behaviors. We must begin to take seriously all of God's creation and how we are responsible for the destruction as well as the care. The reality is climate change is real and it impacts the availability of food for people. It's complicated for us because we are complicit, but we are not without hope.

The good news is there are some things we can do to reduce our complicity. Some are simple; some are more complex. We can consume less. I'm not saying stop buying things, but more is not better. We can recycle. I know that isn't really a thing in Texas apparently, but it is something we can do as a matter of faith. We can eat less meat and more locally grown vegetables and fruits. There are so many things we can do, but doing nothing isn't an option. I know that these small things are not the cure-all for our problems, but they help, and they are a way of practicing our faith as followers of Jesus caring for God's creation.

Today I'm going to do something a little different. Take out the Worship Bulletin and turn to the back where it says "notes." I want you to take a minute and write down one thing you can do to care for God's creation and help improve this planet. Something that you are not doing now or maybe not doing regularly. Write this down and see if you can make that change. For me, I'm going to return to doing meatless Mondays for dinner. You don't have to share your one thing with us unless you like, but write it down. Then I want you to write down one thing that will take much more effort on your part to do that will show care for God's creation and help improve the planet. I want you to pray about this big thing over the next week or so and see if it is something you can in fact do. The lawyer who stood up to try Jesus wanted one easy thing to do one time and be done; Jesus gave him an ongoing "do." We as followers of Jesus have an ongoing "do," so let's go and do likewise.

Not Up in Here! (2 Samuel 20:1–2 CEV; 14–22 NLT)

Rev. Dr. Irie Lynne Session

God empowers certain people to become strategic leaders committed to protecting and preserving their communities. The Black Mambas are an example of such leaders. They are the world's first all-female, anti-poaching unit in South Africa. These women have one goal in mind—saving the rhino from extinction. "The illicit sale of the rhino horn has become one of the most valuable commodities in the world, worth as much as gold, diamonds and cocaine."[22] Greedy and unscrupulous people come into these African communities, hunt, brutalize, and butcher rhinos. Smugglers then leave with their horns to potentially make hundreds of thousands of dollars. It is estimated that in South Africa one rhino is killed every seven hours. To save South Africa's rhinos, game reserves have experimented with various technologies, drones, thermal optics, and satellite tracking. But the only thing that has shown any return on its investment is the Black Mambas movement. These women have specialty training in tracking and bush craft. The Black Mambas is a movement led by a unit of twenty-six women committed to resisting the destruction of their community and its valuable assets.

The #metoo, #churchtoo, and #blacklivesmatter movements are also movements created and led by women to resist patriarchy, white supremacy, and racism. These movements are needed because unfortunately there are those who actually look for opportunities to steal, kill, and destroy the vibrancy and vitality of human beings and communities in order that they might gain profits, prestige, and/or power. Such was the case of Sheba in our preaching passage.

Sheba's Revolt

Sheba staged a revolt against King David and convinced all the people from Israel to follow him. Now before we go further, I need to provide a bit of context so we understand where David's head was at when all this went down. David had just returned to Jerusalem after running for his life. His son Absalom led a rebellion against him. Upon his return to Jerusalem, David learned that Absalom, the son who had him on the run, the son who

22. Williams and Warner, "The Black Mambas."

raped each of his father's concubines on the rooftop of the palace for all Israel to see, had been killed by Joab, the military leader—despite David's instructions to bring Absalom back alive.

Joab—A Bad Man

David returns to Jerusalem only to be met with more drama. Now Sheba wants his throne. But Joab isn't having it! Joab is also the one who conspired with Amnon, another of David's sons, to rape his half sister Tamar. Joab was a bad man, a fierce and ofttimes ruthless military leader. But despite his hot-tempered nature and take-no-prisoners attitude, Joab was loyal to the throne. And so, he set out to find Sheba and handle up on some business.

Sheba in Abel

Sheba and those who joined him in the rebellion took flight. The Bible says Sheba "passed through all the tribes of Israel" until he arrived in the town of Abel, where he found safety, sanctuary, and refuge (2 Samuel 20:14 NLT). The people of Abel were harboring a fugitive and didn't know it. But Joab did. And so, Joab and his brother Abishai pursued Sheba to the town of Abel.

Picture this, Sheba's in hiding in Abel, and Joab and his army have just arrived. It is about to be on and poppin' up in the city. Joab's men begin battering the wall of the city to break it down. They are coming for Sheba! Then something unusual happens. Joab hears a voice. But not just any voice. He hears the voice of a woman! The woman was inside the city of Abel on the other side of wall, but her voice was loud enough for Joab to hear her over the battering of the wall.

She Got Loud

Beloved, there are times when a woman must raise her voice—when we must get loud. Like Alexandria Ocasio-Cortez (AOC), political activist and U.S. congresswoman. I remember when AOC raised her voice as she talked about sexual assault. She raised her voice to the listening crowd, "Sexual assault is not a crime of passion; it's about the abuse of power." She got loud when she said, "It is always women who are marginalized, it is the young, it is the interns, it is the immigrant, it is the trans. They are always most at risk."[23] AOC raised her voice; she got loud. Auntie Maxine raised her voice, "I am reclaiming my time."[24]

We must raise our voices and tell our stories of assault and abuse, even if we're not believed. You see, there's a certain kind of freedom that comes for us when we raise our voices. Freedom from shame. Freedom from the expectations of others. Freedom from injustice.

Following the example of the woman of Abel, there are times when we have to raise our voices—like when our children lie dead in the streets because of the implicit bias of some police officers. We must raise our voices against discrimination, sexism, gender-based violence, and any and everything else that threatens our own well-being and that of our communities. Joab heard the loud voice of a woman. Now, it's one thing for a woman to raise her voice and get loud; it's another for her to actually have something meaningful to say.

Womanist Wisdom Calls Out

The woman of Abel had something to say: "Listen, to me, Joah. Come over here so I can talk to you!" (2 Samuel 20:16 NLT). Joab was called out by a woman who had something important to say. But she wasn't just any woman—the text calls her a "wise woman." I'd like to think this sista had womanist wisdom! Linda Hollies, womanist preacher and author says, "Womanist wisdom is that learned by women of color who have grappled with the issues of race, sex, and class discrimination and yet continue to rise above the odds and the world's expectations. Womanist wisdom gives you a word of sage knowledge. It's not the 'easy' way. But it's the way of courage." Womanist wisdom called Joab out.

Have you ever been called out? You're about to make a foolish move and a friend, parent, or partner sees the mess you're about to make and calls you out. They show you the trouble you're about to cause for yourself? Well, maybe you haven't, but I've been called out a time or two. And, I will confess that I'm grateful for people who saw what I couldn't. I'm grateful for people who loved me enough to tell me the truth.

23. Ocasio-Cortez, "twitter.com@AOC," https://twitter.com/aoc/status/1173609907033116672?lang=en.

24. Waters, "Maxine Waters Teaches," para. 2.

Everyone needs wise women in their life—women who have been through some things and came out more insightful, and less afraid to speak up and out. The woman who called out Joab was a wise woman, most probably a district judge in Abel, a city known for its fair and just judicial system. This woman was a protector of her community and a woman of influence. She was a woman who seemed to understand the rights of her constituency, her community. Which meant, she also knew Joab violated the law by attacking Abel without first seeking peace.

According to the law (Deuteronomy 20:10–12), peace was to be offered before a city was laid waste. According to the rules of war, Joab was to have made a verbal appeal to the city before he attacked it. But he didn't do that. The wise woman in Abel knew what Joab was about to do was a violation of the law. And, she possessed the courage to confront him with that truth—something no man had ever done. By calling Joab out, by talking back to him, bell hooks would argue that in her actions, she positioned herself as "Joab's equal."

It was no small thing that no man ever tried to negotiate with Joab, a fierce, righteous warrior. I imagine Joab wasn't used to being called out. But because she knew the law, she called him out. People, know your rights. Women, know your rights! On your job, know the personnel policies. Know the bylaws, the constitution, and Roberts Rules of Order. You never know when you may need to call someone out, or when you may need to call the system to account. But when you do, you better have your facts straight.

She Interrupted

She called Joab out and when she did, she did something else—she *interrupted* the battering of the wall. Do we have any interrupters in the house tonight? This wise woman was an interrupter.

I recently learned of a group in Chicago called "The Interrupters." They have one goal in mind—to save a life. Their tagline is "to cure it you need to interrupt it." Chicago's Interrupters, through informed conversations, group meetings, and consistent involvement in their respective communities, disrupt violence.

The wise woman in Abel was a violence interrupter. She called out Joab, a man who was about to destroy the community she loved. Can't you see Joab's men looking around wondering, wait what? Did she just call out Joab? Doesn't she know who he is and what he's capable of? Joab killed his own cousin for disobeying a direct order from King David. Did she call *him* out? Why yes, I do believe she did! But listen. It gets even better than that! Joab obliges her strong request; the Bible says that Joab "came near her." Then she asked, "Are you Joab?" And he answered, "I am" (2 Samuel 20:17 NLT).

She Speaks, He Listens

Once she affirms his identity, the wise woman advises Joab, "Listen carefully to your servant." He answered, "I'm listening." Church, can I tell you how much I love reading that part! Joab responded, "I'm listening" (2 Samuel 20:17 NLT).

Oh, how different our world would be if more military leaders said, "I am listening." What if we had more government officials who said to wise women, "I am listening"? What if we had leaders in the White House who, when a wise woman spoke, they responded, "I am listening"? Wouldn't it be healing for someone to say to survivors of intimate partner violence and sexual assault, "I am listening"? What if lawmakers would say to LGBTQ persons and transgender persons, and gender-nonconforming persons, "We are listening"? Joab listened. Joab, the man in charge of the king's army, just as he was about to break through the wall of the city and capture Sheba, stopped what he was doing—laid aside his agenda, his strategic battle plan, and listened to the wise woman of Abel. He didn't try to mansplain his actions; he didn't assert his authority or power to make her feel small; he didn't tell her she was out of place. None of that. Joab listened. She speaks, he listens.

This wise woman explains to Joab the historicity of Abel. How it was known for its wisdom and good judgment. She makes it clear that to destroy Abel was to destroy a city that was "a mother in Israel" (2 Samuel 20:19 CEV). A go-to city for settling disagreements and lawsuits because Abel was known as a city where right judgments always prevailed. The wise woman speaks and Joab listens. He listens to a woman who had the ear of her community, a woman who knew the legal system. A woman of great influence. Joab listens to a wise woman who possessed the courage to confront him and show him the injustice he was about to mete out to innocent people. Joab listens to a wise woman who interrupted a siege, a confident woman who wasn't intimidated by patriarchy, people, politics, or power structures. In this text, the wise woman uses her voice, her critical thinking, and her influence as resistance to the government officials about to destroy her city. This wise woman refuses to be silent or silenced—perhaps she knew, like Zora Neale Hurston, "If you are silent about your pain, they'll kill you and say you enjoyed it."[25] She would not be silent. There was too much at stake for silence. What was at stake? The city, the community—her home, her hood, filled with families, children, friends, businesses, markets, and synagogues.

Communal Concerns

This wise woman had *communal concerns*—she was a protector and preserver of community. She resisted militarism, which would have led to the complete destruction of her community. And she had the influence to rally her community to handle business with the one who put their community at risk.

Many of our communities are at risk. Some are at risk from gentrification; some are already food deserts. Some are at risk of unequal treatment based on race, sexual orientation, and/or gender roles. We can learn a thing or two from the wise woman of Abel, a woman who had in mind the best interest of her city.

I wonder, do our city leaders have in mind the best interest of the people— or just their parts of the city? Recently, the Urban Institute completed a study of 274 cities to determine their economic equity. Out of 274 cities, Dallas ranked 274th, dead last for economic equality.[26] Dallas has the most economic inequity out of 274 cities studied. And yet, business is booming in Dallas. High rises are going up everywhere; upscale apartments are coming in to the Bishop Arts District, a community with a large Hispanic population. City leaders and the wealthy are battering down the walls of Oak Cliff, South Dallas, and other parts of town with a high concentration of poor people. But the wise woman in this text had in mind the best interest of the city and ALL the people who lived within its walls.

25. Hurston, "If You Are Silent," para. 1.

26. Macon, "Dallas Ranked Dead Last," para. 1–2.

Credible and Convincing

Because of her credibility in the community, she knew the people would listen to her just as Joab had. So, she assured Joab that she and the people of the city would deliver the head of Sheba. She wasn't willing to sacrifice an entire city for one scoundrel. Sheba meant the city no good—he was a troublemaker rather than a peacemaker. He entered Abel not with the best interest of the city in mind, but to save his own life, putting the entire city and its people at risk of destruction.

Everyone who comes into our city doesn't have in mind the best interest of that city. Every politician who comes to your church right before an election doesn't have in mind the best interest of your community. And so, the people cut off the head of Sheba and threw it over the wall to Joab.

What do we need to throw over the wall? What do we need to get rid of in our city? Well, I think we need to get rid of monuments to white supremacy. We need to get rid of council persons who don't support earned paid sick leave for Dallas citizens. We need to get rid of politicians who don't think Dallas employees should earn a living wage. We need to throw implicit bias, heterosexism, and gender binaries over the wall. We most certainly need to throw white supremacy, patriarchy, and white fragility over the wall. These things don't make our city better, but worse. They slowly and methodically destroy the possibility for creating beloved community.

Not Up in Here!

So, the wise woman convinced her community to join together, to work in unity, to collaborate to get rid of, throw over the wall that which meant it no good. Joab and the Abel community listened to a credible and convincing wise woman. Now, I have to admit, I was baffled by Joab's humble listening and acquiescence to the wise woman's voice. Joab wasn't typically a man who took advice from anyone, let alone a woman. There were times when Joab didn't even listen to the king! So, why listen to this wise woman? So, I did a little of research and discovered something interesting. The woman of Abel wasn't the first wise woman Joab listened to.

In 2 Samuel, chapter 14, we find Joab calling on the wise woman of Tekoa to assist him in negotiating a truce between David and Absalom. Joab seemed to understand the value of consulting and following the sage wisdom of women. He understood that wise women were able to communicate effectively the fundamental cultural values of their people and their God. Somehow Joab learned that wise women could be trusted because of their strength as diplomats, their depth of instinct, self-possession, and intelligence. It wasn't lost on Joab that wise women were able to handle difficult situations with extraordinary skill, sensitivity, and courage. And so, when the wise woman of Abel used her influence to resist the destruction of her city, when she in essence said, "Not Up in Here," Joab listened.

Whenever a wise woman says, "Not Up in Here," she means it; she's going to protect her people!

When a wise woman says, "Not Up in Here," she's going to hold her country accountable for living into its stated values!

When a wise woman says, "Not Up in Here," she's going to show up and speak up for her children.

When a wise woman says, "Not Up in Here," she's going to protect her family and community.

When wise women say, "Not Up in Here," they're going to save the rhinos in South Africa.

When a wise woman says, "Not Up in Here," she's going to put feet on her faith and follow in the steps of Jesus, who also said, "Not Up in Here"; not even death will have the last word!

Not Up in Here, Up in Here!

Hope in Crossing Borders (Matthew 2:13–15)

Rev. Kamilah Hall Sharp

It seems to me that the birth of Jesus brought forth a lot of talk in the Bethlehem streets. Of course, there was no Twitter back then, but I think Jesus was trending. When the word on the street was that there was a new king in town, this clearly ruffled some feathers, mainly the ones worn by Herod.

See, Herod had been in power for about thirty years. He came to power when the Romans placed him there and no one voted to remove him from office. As with most people with power, Herod enjoyed his power and he was not looking to give it up or even share it with anyone else. Herod would do whatever he thought he needed to do to hold on to power. Herod would lie, Herod would have secret conversations, Herod would be vengeful, Herod would kill babies, and not think twice about any of it in order to maintain his power.

So, to avoid the deception and violence of the one in power, in order to be safe, in order to have peace, Mary and Joseph took Jesus to Egypt. In Egypt they were beyond the reach of Herod. Egypt was seen as a place of refuge, Egypt. Scholarly gentrification and racist interpretation have provided us with a blonde-haired, blue-eyed Jesus, but the reality is Mary and Joseph took their brown-skinned baby boy to Egypt so they could lay low and keep him safe. As the biblical scholar and one of the first Black people to hold a doctorate in biblical studies, the late Cain Hope Felder, says, the parents of sweet baby Jesus followed the established train to Africa, not Europe.[27] They had to go from where they were and cross the border in order for them and their baby to be safe.

I'm amazed at how many people love to talk about the miraculous birth of Jesus but don't want to talk about how his family had to run across the border for their safety. And how Egypt didn't try to keep them from coming. There was no wall to block Jesus from entering Egypt, he didn't have to wait on the Egyptian border in Judea and wait to apply for asylum, and there were no financial requirements. They were allowed to come and find refuge.

You know this story teaches me some things. First of all, when there is no peace where you are, sometimes you may have to cross some borders to find it. There are times when we have to move from where we are in order to protect and/or prepare ourselves for the work that lies ahead. Understanding that what lies ahead is our work and often our hope. Elaine Crawford says, "Hope is the bridge from oppression to liberation."[28] And there are many times when if we do not move, our hope can die or it can be killed in the hands of others, and sometimes it's a slow death.

Here, Joseph and Mary see the hope in Jesus; they heard of the hope in Jesus and now they must make sure that hope lives on. In order to do that, they must cross the border. The thing I realized is they didn't do this on their own. The three Magi first of all showed up. They travelled far to show up and see this baby, and they came bearing gifts. The gifts they brought could be used, and some of them could help pay for their expenses in traveling and living in Egypt. They went into their treasure chest and gave nice gifts because they were investing in the hope that Jesus was bringing. For

27. See Felder, "Cultural Ideology," 194.

28. Crawford, *Hope in the Holler*, xii.

me, that shows support: to show up and invest in hope is how to make sure that hope lives on. This shows us that Mary and Joseph did not do this thing alone. For sure God was with them and other people were working with them to make sure that this hope lived on.

Which is why I am hurt and confused by so much of what happens today. We see people taking the little they have and leaving the country they live in because it is so dangerous. Taking their kids just like Mary and Jesus and trying to cross borders so that they may live. They head for these borders, believing there is some hope on the other side of the border. Yet, we have people who will do anything and everything they can to keep people from crossing the border to get hope. So, we have children being separated from their parents, not being fed, dying as they are held in cages, in camps, and they are told they cannot cross this border. More children on the other side of the border freezing outdoors because they are told they cannot cross this border.

But Mary and Joseph traveled by night and crossed the border and went to Egypt. I'm so glad Herod couldn't stop them at the border, I'm so glad no border patrol could detain them, I'm so glad the wise men supported them, and I'm so glad they had safe passage to Egypt, because there they found refuge. There they crossed the border carrying hope. The hope was not with Herod. The hope was with Mary and Joseph in Egypt. In Egypt, hope lived on even while Herod sought to capture it and destroy it. Hope grew and began to spread. Hope outlasted Herod. And we know that just as Jesus crossed the border, our ancestors crossed borders, and sometimes we might need to cross borders. We know there is a history of hope that continues to live on. So, we too can have hope in all of us because as the Voices of The Gathering sang tonight, "Emmanuel," which means "God is with us." And despite talk about our personal relationships with God, it's not all about us; it's not only about us. God is with us all. And since God is with us, we continue to invest in hope, protect hope, and carry hope forward not just for ourselves, but for others, for those who will come later. Carry forward the hope.

It's All God (Isaiah 5:1–7 CEB)

Rev. Dr. Irie Lynne Session

What God has for you is for you. If you're like me, you've heard this quote plenty of times during your walk with Jesus. The idea is no matter what happens in your life no one can take away what God has for you. Because, it's for YOU. The longer I live, the more I discover about the nature of God, the less I believe that quote as stated. What I have come to believe is this: *What God has for you is not just for you. Not your money. Not your wealth. Not your prosperity. Not your house. Not your car. Not your food. Not your intellect, not even your faith.*

God is not a capitalist. God is not concerned as much about our individual prosperity as our communal thriving and flourishing. Just this week I read a quote by Franklin D. Roosevelt that gets to the heart of what I mean: "The test of our progress is not whether we add more to the abundance of those who have much; it is whether we provide enough for those who have too little."[29]

A Divine Setup

Providing for those who have too little is a concern in tonight's preaching passage. It begins with the prophet Isaiah illuminating what I call a "Divine Setup."

Here's what I mean. God set up Jerusalem to be prosperous and productive in every way. To flourish economically, materially, and spiritually. God made provision for God's own people. God did all the heavy lifting to ensure the community's prosperity. The Bible says that God removed stones from the vineyard. Stones were barriers, obstacles, and enemies—any and everything preventing human flourishing and economic prosperity. In this text, which is actually a poem, Jerusalem is a vineyard, personified as a woman. But what woman? Or rather, which women, since prophets always had communal concerns? A prophetic critique was rarely focused on individual concerns, unless the individual's ungodly behavior adversely affected the community. In this text, there is a communal concern that Jerusalem as a vineyard, as a well-kept woman, failed to produce what was expected. In fact, Isaiah 1:21 gets even more ratchet. It describes Jerusalem as a town

29. Roosevelt, "Second Inaugural Address," para. 29.

that "has become a prostitute! She was full of justice; righteousness lived in her—but now murderers" (CEB).

Can I keep it real? And, I don't like it. I don't like it one bit. I know women whose backs are against the wall. Women who don't have money. Women who don't have pensions. Women who don't have wealthy parents. Women whose options are limited. Women who were not set up like Jerusalem, as vineyard as women. This metaphor brought to mind women I've ministered to for years. Women with sugar daddies and sugar mamas. It represents, at least to me, this capitalistic idea of "I'll do this for you—spend my money on you, give you clothes, cars, and cash—if you do this"—fill in the blank—"for me."

Thus, as a womanist interpreter of this metaphor of Jerusalem as *vineyard as women,* I bring critique to bear on not just any women, but women of means, chosen women. Women protected and provided for, women whose husbands were at the top of the social pyramid.

Women of Means

"Women of means" is the metaphor I lift up to represent the ones who by this world's standards have economic, social, and material prosperity who fail to use said prosperity and privilege to dismantle oppressive systems and structures. During ancient times that would have been kings, priests, government and army officials, and land owners—the ruling elites of Judah and Israel.[30] Today, that might be the 53 percent who chose whiteness over their gender. Today that would be the owner of the Miami Dolphins, Stephen Ross, who has a nonprofit supposedly championing racial equality and who had a recent fundraiser for 45 that yielded $12 million for his re-election campaign. As Miami Dolphins wide receiver Kenny Stills commented, "It just doesn't add up."

Twenty-First Century Setup

This Isaiah passage deals with what we do with what God has graciously provided. What we do with our money and prosperity. In this text God as the creator and cultivator of the vineyard set it up to prosper. In the twenty-first century there are people, God's people, who are also set up. Some are

30. Chaney, "Whose Sour Grapes?" 105–22.

set up because they were born into a setup family—they didn't work for it; they didn't earn it. They were born into it. Others are set up because they had opportunity to use their God-given gifts, intellect, and skill to set up themselves and their family members. But, no matter how some are set up, no matter how we arrive at a place of flourishing and prosperity, there are human beings on the other end of the prosperity spectrum. There are God's beloveds who are not flourishing. The question then becomes, what of those who are not set up?

The Prosperous Prevent the Poor from Prospering.

No Unrealistic Expectations

Just as it was then, so it is today. God has expectations of those who have prospered. And, God does not have unrealistic expectations. God has expectations of fidelity, fruitfulness, and flourishing. Sadly, God's expectations are often not met. Why? Because too often the prosperous prevent the poor from also prospering. Too many prosperous believers use God's provisions to exploit and oppress others of God's human creation. Womanist biblical scholar Delores Williams asked this question of this Isaiah text that must be interrogated, "What happens when systems are set up that prevent the growth of good grapes? What happens when prosperous people use what God has provided just for themselves?"[31]

My Response:

- What happens when we see "the land of the free and home of the brave" as belonging only to a certain demographic? This is what happens: We see 680 Latinx workers arrested by ICE while their children are in school.
- What happens when prosperous people use what God has intended for all, just for themselves? This is what happens: We get more and more charitable donations for tax deductions and no structural or systemic change.
- What happens when prosperous people use what God has provided just for themselves? This is what happens: We get no increased restrictions on gun sales. Restrictions that could save countless lives.

31. Williams, "The Salvation of Growth," 899.

Live Up to God's Expectations

I wonder, what would it look like if followers of Jesus put forth every effort to use our money and prosperity to live up to God's expectations that we bring about justice and righteousness? What is justice? What is biblical justice? Here it is: As a primary attribute of God, justice is "maintaining the right relationship to the poor and the destitute, rescuing the weak and the needy, and delivering them from the hand of the wicked" (Psalm 82:3–4 author paraphrase).

In the Hebrew, a term used to describe the justice of God is *misphat* and refers to creating or maintaining equitable, fair, and harmonious social relationships. *Misphat* suggests that every human being is created in the image of God and therefore, "has the same inalienable right to abundance and wholeness and freedom from oppression."[32]

What if each and every one of us strived to help God get the world that God wants? You see, I am clear of one thing: a day of reckoning is coming. God has expectations. God will get what God wants. Even if God has to destroy/uproot/dismantle the vineyard to do so.

But I don't think it has to come to that.

It's All God's

What if everything we had, we saw as belonging to God. All that money some of y'all have in the bank. That Mercedes! That Maybach! That Lexus! That Toyota! What if you saw that intellectual mind you are cultivating in college or graduate school as a gift from God? What if we really believed those hands that create technology, skyscrapers, and cages to house children were given us by God? Today, let's give that idea a try. Starting today, our mind belongs to God. Our eyes belong to God. Our feet belong to God. Our hands belong to God. Our money belongs to God. Today, it's all God. God enabled us to earn it, make it, build it, and buy it. It's All God!

Jesus knew it too. That's why he said on one occasion, "I have come down from heaven not to do my will, but the will of him who sent me" (John 6:38 CEB). So, "Let the same mind be in [us] that was in Christ Jesus, who, though he was in the form of God, did not regard equality with God as something to be exploited, but emptied himself" (Philippians 2:5–7a NRSV). Jesus humbled himself. Let us go and do likewise.

32. Hendricks, *The Politics of Jesus*, 43.

Last Sunday morning I walked into worship at Friendship-West Baptist Church a little late. As I went to my seat, the male chorus was singing "It's All God,"[33] a song I never heard before. I've since done a Google search of the song, sung by The Soul Seekers. Listening to "It's All God" again, I thought, "This is the title of my sermon."

Thank You for Being a Friend (Luke 5:17–20)

Rev. Kamilah Hall Sharp

Anyone who knows me knows that at the end of the day I like to get on my couch with my snacks and my lap quilt to watch *The Golden Girls*. This is how I relax. I've seen probably every episode; I will finish the lines with the characters, and still laugh at the jokes. Most of us have a favorite show that we love to watch over and over, and that one is mine. *The Golden Girls* has one of the most memorable opening songs on a television show. As soon as I hear it, I immediately know what it is, but if you ever pay attention to the lyrics of the song, they are actually pretty good. "Thank you for being a friend. Travel down the road and back again. Your heart is pure, you're a pal and a confidant."

For me, this is a great way of thinking about a true friend. Someone you can count on to be there with you through the changes of life because we all have changes in life. When things are going well, they celebrate with you. And when things are not going well, they are there because sometimes we find ourselves in situations where we need help. We need a friend.

Women throughout this country and the world have found themselves in these rough situations as they suffer abuse verbally and through slaps, punches, kicks at the hands of someone who claims to love them. The boyfriend, girlfriend, partner, or husband is determined to have power over them and desires to control them, so they become abusive. Our girls, women, and sometimes men could use a friend but may find themselves often in a situation feeling alone because they have been isolated from their friends and family by an abuser. And for one to find themselves in this situation is not easy to understand, because people don't want to be abused, people don't seek to be abused, and most of us think it will never happen to me. Until it does.

33. Lilly, "It's All God."

Domestic violence does not just happen to certain women. Domestic violence and intimate partner violence happen to all types of people no matter race, social class, and even gender. Though most who suffer abuse are women, there are men and nonbinary people who are abused as well. But the hard reality for us is that Black women are 30 to 50 percent more likely to be victims to domestic violence than white women. Black women are more likely to suffer through domestic violence and are statistically less likely to report than any other ethnicity.

There are many reasons why we do not report abuse. First of all, let's be honest; most of us don't trust the police. The police have not been known in our community to protect Black and brown bodies. And Black women have been ignored by police when they call and even end up in jail or dead themselves after calling the police for help. Some of us don't report because of the shame we feel. Then some of us don't ask for help because we have internalized the need to be strong. We have the "Strongblackwoman" syndrome we've talked about before, all pushed together, no room to breathe. And the "Strongblackwoman" syndrome can leave us feeling like we have nowhere to turn to and so we do not report. The person who is being abused can be our neighbor, relative, or even us, and it's happening all around us daily.

Just this past week here in Dallas, Donna Alexander, a domestic violence advocate and the young entrepreneur who created the Anger Room, was reported to have been beaten to death by either her live-in or estranged boyfriend. So, on today we speak her name; we could spend hours calling the names of those who have been murdered by someone who professes to love them. We have many women, children, and men living in danger.

And what I believe is a person who is being abused or stalked could use a friend, a friend like the ones in our passage today. Here Luke reports that the friends of this paralyzed man take their friend to Jesus so he can be healed. This text is fascinating to me because it shows so clearly what friends in community with faith can accomplish with Jesus.

When I look at this passage and the friends who brought their paralyzed friend to Jesus, it speaks to me. The first thing I noticed is the friends knew that their friend needed help. Now in this case it was easy to see that he needed help because he was paralyzed; his issue was clearly visible. The thing about domestic violence and intimate partner abuse is sometimes we don't see it because everything appears normal. Because there is no one type of abuse victim, often people who are being abused and we have no idea. And then when someone is killed, we hear a lot of "I cannot believe it" or "he was so nice." These are words you hear in cases like Karen Smith, who was killed by her husband, Cedric Anderson, who was a pastor and called "a man of God" by those commenting after her murder. Yes, there are times when we do not see someone is in need and we never suspect anything is wrong.

Then there are times when we do, yet we pretend not to see. We notice the bruise on the face. We see the extra makeup. We hear the violent arguments, but we tell ourselves that's none of our business. There are times when we can see that a person is in danger and in need, and yet we turn our heads to look the other way. The friends in this passage who knew their friend needed help did not turn the other way; they instead went and picked him up to get him some help.

You know the other thing is the friends in the passage were informed. They knew where Jesus was, so they knew where to go for help. They knew if they took their friend to Jesus, he could get the help he needed. If we as a community are going to be the friend people need in these times, we have to be informed. We have to know where to direct or take people for the help. Now I can hear somebody saying we got to get them to Jesus. Yes, and we have to get them to people and places here that can help them and keep them safe, which requires us to be educated on some things. There is some information we need to know if we are to help others escape abuse.

I know many of us have said it before, "If it was me, I would just leave." Maybe we would and maybe we wouldn't. A lot of times we like to say what we will do in a certain situation when we have never been in that situation, and it's easy to say "do something" when it doesn't require our doing. As Rev. Freddie Haynes has said, "We judge people's actions and we don't know their options."[34] We will say they just need to leave, but that does not take seriously what that can mean. See, for those who are in an abusive relationship, leaving can be dangerous.

The sad reality is that often it is when people leave that the abuser tries to kill them. Leaving can be difficult because domestic violence is about control. Often the person being abused may not have access to money, resources, and documents, so up and leaving really is not that simple. There has to be a plan to leave, but to be the kind of friend that a person in this situation would need we need to know that. We need to know where they can get the help they need. We need to know what they should and should not do. We have to be informed.

34. Haynes, "Headlights or Taillights."

You know the friends in the passage also took a risk to help their friend. Think about it; they were so determined to get their friend to help that they took him to the roof of the house, made a hole in the roof, and lowered their friend down so that they could put him before Jesus. You have to understand; this was not a home that had to pass inspection before it could be occupied. Houses in this time were not made like ours today. But really, would we want to climb on the roof of a home even today and stand up there while putting a hole in the roof? That's dangerous. And we cannot be honest about helping those affected by domestic violence without recognizing it can be dangerous.

I don't believe it does us any good to tell people about things like domestic violence if we aren't going to tell the whole story. There is a reason that the locations of safe homes for domestic violence victims are kept secret. There is a reason when people do leave they don't want them to know where they are, because this person has already showed they have the ability to hurt other people. So, let's be real, this can be dangerous. And I believe we have a responsibility to do what is right even though often doing what is right comes with risk. Ask Harriet, ask Mandela, ask Cesar Chavez, ask Coretta Scott King. We have to do what is right even when it's risky.

But these friends were willing to take that risk because they believed it would help their friend; they believed the risk would pay off because they believed Jesus could help them and they were right. These folks had so much faith in the ability of Jesus to help that they would not let the crowds keep them from him, they would not let the difficulty keep them from him, and they would not let the risk keep them from getting their friend the help. What kind of faith is that?

I also thought a lot about the paralyzed man. Here he is unable to walk around freely, depending on others, and being marginalized because in this society most people believed if something was wrong with you, it was because you sinned. You did something wrong or your parents did something wrong. The pain one must feel to have been told the only reason this is happening to you is because of what you did wrong. The pain one must feel when they internalize this and begin to believe it. Here he is living with this, and his friends now are taking him to get help. The text does not say whose idea it was. I don't know if the man asked them or if it was the friends' idea. What I do know is the friends are now taking him. That tells me two things: (1) The friends had to be willing to take him, and (2) the man had to be willing to go. The friends had to be willing to take him, and the man had to be willing to go.

See, what that means for us is as a community we have to be willing to help those in need and those of us who have been abused must be willing to take help. What would it look like if we were the friends lowering our sister before Jesus? What would it look like if we came as a community around our people in need and said, "My friend, I got you in this time of need"? How does the church create a space where people feel safe and comfortable enough to come and say, "I need help; I'm in danger"?

For so long, we have failed victims of domestic violence. Abused women have been counseled to pray for their abuser to stop, try not to make them mad, and stay. Well, do I pray before or after I'm beaten? Or they are told, "Don't get divorced because as 'Christians' we should not get a divorce." My friends, we have lost too many people to that type of damaging counsel. Please hear me when I say this; I do not believe God wants any of us to stay in a relationship where we are being abused, married or not. I believe God loves us too much to want us to be abused. God does not want what God has created and said is wonderfully and fearfully made harmed in any way. And as the church, as followers of Jesus, we should not want anyone to be abused for the sake of staying married or in a relationship. If someone comes to us and is willing to receive our help and says, "I need help," we must be willing to help them. We have to be able to get people to the help they need.

Unfortunately, too often we have failed in churches in getting people the help they need because we tell them things like, "All you need is Jesus." Well, what if I got Jesus and I'm still getting beat? We sing songs like, "As long as I got King Jesus I don't need nobody else." See, we have been conditioned to say we just need Jesus. I am not standing before you today saying we don't need Jesus. I need Jesus, we all need Jesus, and I believe we still need each other and there are some physical things we need to survive. Telling someone in need they just need Jesus isn't enough. Really, it's a cop-out for us. It's a way of us not really getting involved. I think we sometimes forget we are the hands and feet of Jesus. We can show or take people to get the help they need. We can take them to shelters, provide them with resources and the things they need for help, and we can bring them to Jesus to get them what they need to heal. Because the wounds of domestic violence go much further than the cuts and bruises on the skin. Domestic violence also can wound the spirit. I often say "mind, body, and spirit," and this is truly a situation where one needs support for their mind, body, and spirit.

When the friends in this passage bring the man to Jesus, he's so moved by their faith he tells him his sins are forgiven. You know I want to make sure we understand this in context because context matters. As I said before, in this particular time sickness was related to sin in the minds of most people. They thought if something was wrong with you, it was because of some sin you did. If we're honest about it, a lot of us still think like that although it's not true. And I want to make it abundantly clear to those who have experienced domestic violence or intimate partner violence: it is not because you have sinned. It is not because you have done something wrong. Jesus tells him his sins are forgiven. I really believe that was for the people around who were listening.

When Jesus says this, it causes a commotion because they want to know who was he to forgive sins? But here is where Jesus is able to show his power when as a rebuttal to their interrogation he tells the man to stand up and walk. You see that is where I felt the spirit of God moving. Jesus told this man who could not walk, who was paralyzed, and could not even get to Jesus without the help of friends who were determined to get him to Jesus to get some help. He told that man to stand up and walk. And the man stood up and walked.

See, I believe right now God is saying to us, "Stand up and walk." To my people who may be in an abusive relationship, "Stand up and walk. It's all right to get help; there is help available so stand up and walk." To the survivor of abuse who knows what it's like and can help guide a friend to safety, "Stand up and walk. Reach back and pull another friend to safety." To the person who knows that their friend or family member is abusing someone, "Stand up and walk. Say something because abuse thrives in silence; people are dying while nothing comes from our mouths, so stand up and walk." To the person who may be abusing someone, "Stand up and walk. Walk away and seek professional help and some time with Jesus." To the church, "Stand up and walk." We can no longer ignore the pain of those in need. We can't continue to allow our girls, women, and men to be beaten and killed by those claiming to love them. Silence is violence. Speak up even if your voice shakes. Stand up and walk!

It is time for the church to be a friend to those we've ignored for too long, those who sit in our pews week after week and have to go home and live in terror. It's time for the church to be a friend so people can get the help and healing they need. It's time for the church to stand up and walk! We are the church. Not this building, not The Gathering, not the preachers, but each and every one of us is the church. So, it's time for us to stand up and walk because I believe that's what Jesus has instructed us to do. But the good news is we don't have to walk alone. Not only can we walk together in community, but we can walk with Jesus. And I am so glad that Jesus will walk with us every step of the way. See, I know we got a friend in Jesus, but will we be a friend?

The Silence of Freedom (Acts 16:16–19; Luke 4:18–19)

Rev. Dr. Irie Lynne Session

What does it mean to be ministers of reconciliation in a world torn apart by grief, greed, anger, and hatred?

In church and society all voices do not have freedom of expression. Some voices are privileged while others are silenced. However, ministers of reconciliation understand that God invites all voices to the Table; none are to be silenced. Jesus' ministry of liberating the oppressed and setting the captives free must, therefore, inform our ministries.

God spoke. "Let us make human beings in our image, make them reflecting our nature so THEY can be responsible for (reign over, have dominion over) the fish in the sea, the birds in the air, the cattle, and, yes, Earth itself, and every animal that moves on the face of the earth. God created human beings; God created them godlike, [that is] reflecting God's nature. God created THEM male and female" (Genesis 1:26–27 author paraphrase). In the beginning there was no hierarchy; even God *walked with* human beings. So, whenever a woman is subordinated based on her gender, race, or whatever, she's going to feel some way about it. Something in her will demand freedom; she will cry freedom; she will sing freedom; she will write her freedom; she will blog and text freedom; she will shout for freedom. Because, fundamentally, she was not created to be controlled, dominated, or exploited. She was created to be free. Free to be authentic. Free to become all God intended her to be and to do.

Meant for Freedom

Human beings were meant for freedom, all human beings. Jesus reminds us of this truth in his mission to proclaim release to the captives, to open the eyes of the blind, and to let the oppressed go free. Freedom is the beginning, middle, and the end of becoming who we are created to be. Unless we have the freedom to be who we are, not who people say we are, not who our families want us to be, not who we think we should be, but who we are, unless we have the freedom to be who we are, that is, who God created us to be, we will live beneath our privilege. You see, as my clergy colleague Michelle Shackelford says, "Freedom has life and freedom gives life. It has its own pulse and air. It is the ability to exist exactly as GOD made us." So many of us are spending our lives trying to be someone other than who God dreamed us to be. Without it, without freedom human beings are stifled from creativity, held prisoner to a life we were never meant to live. Such was the case of the unnamed slave girl in our focus text.

Paul and his companions while on their way to prayer meeting, while on their way to church, became acquainted with an exploited teen girl. They didn't just run into her; they learned who she was. They knew her backstory; they knew she was a victim of exploitation. Paul and his companions met a slave girl whose value was tied to what she could produce; they met an unnamed girl, a nameless girl, who at that very moment was being trafficked by hustlers; she was a victim whose gifts had been monetized. Now, I know some translations call her unique ability a "demon." Some call it a "spirit." I call it a "gift." The enslaved girl had a gift, one that enabled her to "tell the future."

Whatever the source of her unusual gift, it is clear that her owners were exploiting her abilities for their own gain. The girl and her gift had fallen into the wrong hands. Is there anybody in here whose gifts have fallen into the wrong hands? When our gifts fall into the wrong hands, we're abused, mistreated. When our gifts fall into the wrong hands, we're exploited, controlled, and manipulated. The enslaved girl and her gift were in the hands of unscrupulous men.

And yet, something within her anticipated release from their captivity. Something within her would not keep silent. That something within was loud, it was persistent, and it angered Paul!

Day after day the slave girl followed Paul and his companions, shouting. So much so that Paul became annoyed. In fact the text says that Paul became "exasperated" (Acts 16:18 NLT). "Exasperated" is a strong word.

"Exasperated" means Paul wasn't merely ticked off; he was irritated, incensed, and infuriated. Paul was mad as_ _ _. Paul was emotionally frustrated, sick and tired of hearing her voice. So, in his frustration, not in his compassion for her, not in his desire to free her from bondage, not in his desire to heal what was broken in her, but because he was exasperated, he exorcised the gift out of her. Because *he* was irritated, he silenced the noise of her shout. Don't you find it interesting that it wasn't until the slave girl became a nuisance to Paul that he loosed her from the control of her traffickers? Her oppression had become an inconvenience to him.

Sadly, it seems that until the freedom of the powerful is *inconvenienced* by the oppression of the marginalized, they will remain silent and impotent. Sometimes we've got to speak up! Sometimes we've got to shout it out! Sometimes we've got to talk about it. Sometimes we must move out of the comfort zones of silence.

If the slave girl had remained silent, she would have remained in bondage; had she not persistently made her presence known to the one who had the power to transform her situation, she would've stayed a slave. Protests, sit-ins, die-ins, strikes, marches, and boycotts are inconveniences for the privileged and powerful, but for the oppressed and the marginalized, these are our last-ditch efforts at seeking justice and liberation. It's only when the oppression of one group adversely impacts the freedom of another group that change comes.

Beloved, freedom isn't typically handed to us on a silver platter. In the words of Afeni Shakur, "Freedom ain't free."[35] It must be wrested from the grips of those who oppress, because they won't let it go willingly.

The Silence of Freedom

The slave girl obtained her freedom because she was an irritant and a nuisance. But the text is silent about her freedom! What happened to her after losing the ability to tell the future? Was she discarded? No longer useful. Was she thrown away? Who was she anyway? Did she have a family to go back to? Was she able to provide for herself? Because of Paul's exorcism, was she now subordinated to a status of triple marginalization—female, formerly incarcerated, and jobless? Was her situation made worse?

35. Shakur, "Key Themes," para. 16.

The slave girl was set free from her captors. But we don't hear any more about her anywhere in the biblical text. They didn't hear about her freedom in Capernaum. They didn't hear about it in Ephesus.

While preparing this sermon, I asked my daughter this question: "Is it possible to be free and oppressed at the same time?" Here was her response: "Yes, it's called being Black." The slave girl in the text, like Black women and girls in the twenty-first century, was free and oppressed at the same time. Just like with the hundreds of Black women and girls who go missing every year, her exorcism didn't make the news. Freedom is yet silent for Black women and girls.

As I look around this room, I see women who've come to realize and embrace their freedom to live into their authentic selves. Women who now have the freedom, in one way or another, to use their Holy Spirit-endowed gifts of preaching, teaching, and other forms of ministerial service. As I'm overwhelmed with excitement for each of you, I can't help but notice who's not in the room. Freedom is yet silent for Black women and girls. We are witnesses that it is indeed possible to be free and oppressed simultaneously. That's why the thought came to the mind of my daughter, a millennial young Black woman, because it's her truth too. But, all too often Black women's truth is denied.

When Black women's truth is denied, our reality is questioned. When Black women's truth is denied, those who rape us go free—for we're still considered "unrapeable." When Black women's truth is denied, white fragility deliberately silences us in the workplace; when Black women's truth is denied, we're stereotyped as "angry Black women." When Black women's truth is denied, our confidence is described as arrogance; when Black women's truth is denied, our intellectual genius is intimidating to the insecure, and somehow their hurt feelings are our fault. When Black women's truth is denied, white women's tears have incredible power. When Black women's truth is denied, we are "preferably unheard."[36] Zora Neale Hurston says it this way, "If you're silent about your pain, they'll kill you and say you enjoyed it."[37] But in response, Black poet and social activist Audre Lorde declares, "Your silences will not protect you."[38]

36. Roy, "The 2004 Sydney Peace Prize," para. 4.

37. Hurston, "If You Are Silent," para. 1.

38. Lorde, "Your Silences," para. 1.

Black Women's Gifts

What would it look like if Black women's truth were believed? What would it look like if our prophetic utterances were taken seriously?

What is missing in the body because of our silencing? Well for one, Black women and other women of color have what scholars call an "epistemological advantage." Marginalized groups are socially situated in ways that make it more possible for us to be aware of things and ask questions than it is for the non-marginalized. The term describes the ways in which Black women and other women of color are able to have a much clearer understanding of how the power structure works within a given society because we are not members of the dominant group.

What else is missing?

Well, Melissa Harris-Perry articulates that Black women are the canaries in the coal mines of society.[39] "To be a 'canary in a coal mine' means that one is so sensitive to environmental conditions that one's suffering sends a warning signal to others nearby. This expression comes from the practice of using canaries as alarms in mining tunnels. The canary's lungs were so delicate that it would be affected by toxic gases and die."[40] I am a canary. It's dangerous to be a canary.

Finally, I maintain that Black women come equipped with thermal imaging cameras—we see the fire in the walls. But all too often our truth is denied. I wonder what would it look like if church and society believed us, validated our truth, and celebrated our gifts.

Freedom from Silence

It is clear that in church and society all voices do not have freedom of expression. Some voices are privileged while others are deliberately silenced. However, ministers of reconciliation understand that God invites all voices to the Table; none are to be silenced. Jesus' ministry of liberating the oppressed and setting the captives free must, therefore, inform our ministries.

As ministers of reconciliation we must create opportunities for the deliberately silenced to be heard. The silenced are the marginalized and oppressed. The silenced are missing from boardrooms and Communion tables.

39. Harris-Perry, *Sister Citizen*, 16.

40. Simpson, "Black Women Must Be More," para. 1.

The silenced are absent from pulpits and coed classrooms. The silenced have a perspective that the privileged and dominant culture does not.

Our freedom doesn't have to be silent. Jesus came to proclaim release to the captives, open the eyes of the blind, and set the oppressed free, and that means all of us. That means every human being on the planet is worthy of freedom. Living into their full human potential. Nelson Mandela said it like this, "For to be free is not merely to cast off one's chains, but to live in a way that respects and enhances the freedom of others."[41] Which is why all of us must work together for the freedom of the oppressed, marginalized, thrown away, and disenfranchised. God has set us free in Christ to work for the freedom of others.

When You Feel Like the Canaanites (Joshua 6:15–21)

Rev. Kamilah Hall Sharp

Tonight we are in another familiar passage that has been told, preached, and sung about many times. The passage tells the story of Joshua leading the people of Israel as they begin their conquest of the land of Canaan. It is here that they follow the instructions of God and march around the city of Jericho seven times, blow the trumpets, shout, and the walls around the city fall down.

We have probably heard some sermons on this passage. We have likely heard celebration of the miracle God performs in making the walls fall down. It is a miraculous event. We celebrate the victory at Jericho. Like the song, "Joshua fit the battle of Jericho and the walls come tumbling down, hallelujah." We shout about the walls tumbling down usually because we want to see the walls in our own life come tumbling down. We want to see God work miracles in our lives once again. We want the victory.

But can I be honest with y'all? Can I be real? This is one of the stories in the Bible that really bothers me. It bothers me for so many reasons. One reason I'm bothered is that when the walls came tumbling down, there were people who lived inside that wall and lives were taken and their world was destroyed without mercy. I think about the women, men, and children who lived inside of Jericho's walls, whose parents and grandparents lived inside Jericho's walls. I can imagine them inside the city living their life as any

41. Mandela, "A Selection of Quotes," para. 11.

other day and hearing horns, hearing shouting, and then for the walls of the city to suddenly collapse. How terrifying must that have been?

I think about the pain and anguish they must have felt to see the walls of the home they have always known to crumble before their eyes, everything around them being destroyed, and then to be attacked. I struggle with how they must have felt. I know we usually don't focus on the Canaanites because we usually read the passage as if we are the Israelites. It is the way we have been taught to read the Bible as Christians and especially as people who have suffered much oppression of our own. I know we are looking for our victory. I know we like to shout for the victory. I know we want to be on the side of the winners in the story, but sometimes that's not really our story.

See, sometimes life is moving fast and seems to be circling us seven times. Sometimes the walls seem to be shaking because our world appears as if it's about to come crashing down. There are days, weeks, and seasons in our lives when we can't really identify with the victor because life seems to be beating us to no ends and we seem to be losing the battle. If we are honest, there are a lot of times when we feel like the Canaanites. Maybe I shouldn't say "we." Maybe your days are filled with sunshine and rainbows; maybe the storms of life have passed over you and moved to the lives of others. Maybe you're just living your best life and if that is your story, that's fine. Praise be to God for your story.

For those of us who have had to go through some things, like when the doctor calls and says the test results aren't normal. Or one minute things seem to be going well and then, bam, your marriage is on the rocks. When you get let go from your job and the little savings you had has run out, but the bills keep coming. When you've been applying for jobs and no one is calling you back. When the car breaks down and you got enough money to either pay rent or get the car fixed, you can't do both. When your mama gets sick and you have to take care of her, your family, and try to keep your job. I'm just talking about the stuff in our day-to-day lives. This does not include the attacks of widespread oppression, the "isms," the foolishness of politicians, or the trauma of being in the world. When life just keeps coming and coming and you feel like you can't take no more. There are times when it feels like the walls are tumbling down and we are being attacked. God, what is really going on?

And that's the other thing that bothers me about this passage. You see, Joshua tells them God has given them this land, God said to go into this land that is already occupied by people, kill them, and we gone keep the gold and the land. I have a problem with that and it troubles my spirit. It troubles me on so many levels. I have a problem with God promising people land that is already occupied by other people. Why couldn't God give them land that was empty? And why would God say kill all these people? I have a problem with this here God. I know many of us were taught it's in the Bible, so it must be OK. Well, for me, I'm sorry, for me it's not all right. I have questions and issues with this, so I have to push back. I know we like to get to the shout so we read past the atrocities to get to the shout, but that can be dangerous. We might need to hold the shout for a minute.

See, because people come centuries later and take this same passage to justify going into lands that were already occupied by people and killing the indigenous people and taking their land and everything they want in it, claiming that it was justified by God. Here in this country when the Puritans arrived and there were people here already in this land, the Puritans read themselves into the text and believed they were the New Israelites and this was their land, Manifest Destiny. Robert Warrior tells how Puritan preachers called Native Americans "Amalekites and Canaanites," which meant if they could not be converted, they were to be annihilated.[42] Those were the preachers.

Just like the story of Canaan, the U.S. conquest narratives are of devastating warfare initiated and perpetrated by the invaders claiming to be authorized by God. Many indigenous people have been murdered and pushed off their land not only here but around the world as colonizers read themselves into this narrative. We have to be careful reading ourselves into the narratives, especially when lives are at stake.

See, the Israelites believed that God had given them this land. The passage we read tonight tells this event from their point of view. But what I know is there is always more than one side of a story. We have to remember what many of us call the Old Testament comes from Hebrew Scriptures, and it tells the story of a people and their relationship with God. The stories written are told from those who were part of this group, and I'm sure the story would look different if told from the perspective of someone else. When you look at this the way it is written, it tells the story as if the Canaanite lives do not matter. Well, God, what about the Canaanites? Don't you care for these people you also created? If told from the Canaanites' point of view, this story could look a whole lot different.

42. Warrior, "Canaanites, Cowboys, and Indians," 264.

See, I've said it before and I'll say it again; when others tell your story, it often does not sound like your story anymore. When we are being attacked by life, being oppressed, at some point we still have to tell our own story, talk about our own experiences and relationship with God. If you can muster up the strength to speak while you're in the midst of your own hell, tell the story. If you can't find the words until after it is over, tell the story. If you lost some people you loved along the way, tell the story. When you had victories, tell the story.

In our lives we all have our own experiences with God that shape our theology, what we think about God and what we believe about God. This can become even more influential in times of our suffering. There are things that you have learned to be true about God that you only know because of what you've been through. And that's the part we must tell. M. Shawn Copeland says a theology of suffering in womanist perspective remembers and retells the lives and suffering of those who came through and those who have gone on. By remembering and retelling our story, we make sure folks understand that our lives do matter not only to us but to God. And that we know God in our own way.[43]

The other thing I kept thinking about while I wrestled with this text is the people in Jericho. When they got attacked, it was not one person in that community who went through that ordeal alone. I don't want y'all to miss that. When the people of Jericho got attacked, it was not one person in that community who went through that alone. See when it hits the fan and gets real tough, a lot of us like to withdraw; we try to go figure out how to get through it alone. The problem with that is it cuts us off from the very community who can try to help, hold us, and if necessary fight back with us.

We are all by ourselves trying to make it and thinking we're the only person going through right now. Let me help somebody, let me help myself, you're not the only one. It's a whole lot of other folk who have gone through what you're going through, going through what you're going through, or maybe gonna end up going through what you going through. True, this is your trouble right now, but it's not a new trouble. What would it look like if instead of trying to do it all by ourselves and pretend like everything is OK, we let the folks in our community know we need help? What could happen if we stood beside each other to face the attacks of life and the world?

The other thing about this story, again I struggled with it all week, then it finally hit me; Kamilah, this ain't the whole story. This is not only

43. Copeland "Wading Through Many Sorrows," 109–129, 123.

one view of the story; it is only part of a bigger story. Whatever happened the day the wall came tumbling down in Jericho wasn't the end of the story either. The story of the Canaanites kept going after that. Even if their story isn't heard enough, the story still did not end that day. Y'all looking at me like how do I know? I know because, first of all, Judges tells how there were Canaanites who lived with Israelites. But then hundreds of years later Mark writes about a Canaanite woman with a clapback.

Y'all remember the Canaanite woman who asked Jesus for help and Jesus tried to play her. Jesus called her a dog, but that didn't stop this Canaanite woman. See, the clapback was real. She let Jesus know this is not how this story will end. She told Jesus to his face, "My life and my daughter's life matters. We matter." She made sure that he understood that they were not going to be ignored and written out of the story. She was going to make sure that he understood, and she helped Jesus on that day (Matthew 15:21–28).

And I believe that she helped us all on that day. Not only did she declare our lives matter and you will see me, but she let us know there was more to the story. See, we have to understand that even when the walls seem to be falling down all around us, nothing seems to be going right, God don't seem to be present, and we believe we might be facing our end, we have to remember this ain't the end of the story. Now let me be clear, it could be an end of a chapter, but it's not the end of the story. I need to know y'all are getting what I'm trying to say.

See, y'all know I love to read. Unfortunately, lately none of my reading has been reading for pleasure, but I love to read all types of books—novels, biographies, books on theology, books on history. Now my daughter is beginning to enjoy reading much more too, which I love. As she got better with reading, she transitioned from short stories to chapter books. The short stories often tell a story in a very little time that typically has a happy ending. Not that they are all fairy tales, but they often end on a high note. Well, now she is in chapter books and what she is learning is all types of things can happen in one chapter. Sometimes things happen to characters, sometimes there are funny parts, or really sad things, sometimes the chapter ends with a cliff-hanger, and some chapters are better than other chapters. The thing is this is just what's going on in that particular chapter.

Our lives are like this. We have chapters of our lives when things couldn't get any better. Everything is going well; life is great. We also have chapters when some of the characters are taken out of our story in different ways, there are plots and twists that we don't see coming, or a particular painful chapter that seems to be going on for such a long time that it seems like this is the way the story is going to end. But truth is it's a chapter, not the whole story, or the end of the story. Just as the Canaanite story did not end when the walls came tumbling down, ours will not either.

Here's the thing, for this story to keep going we have to remember our stories are tied together. And because our stories are tied together, we have to remember this is not a short story that will quickly end on a high note; this story has many chapters, bad and good. Even when I'm in the worst chapter of my life, it's not the whole story. And the chapter of my story can have an impact on the chapters of your story. It doesn't matter if my chapter is good or bad, it can impact your chapter and we can help each other in our chapters. We must share in our bad chapters and our good chapters. See, I believe God is wrapped up in the story of all people. We have to ask ourselves how do we see God in our story? How do we see God in the story of others?

When A Man Loves A Woman (Matthew 1:18–25 CEB)

Rev. Dr. Irie Lynne Session

This Is What Love Does

Tomorrow is the fourth Sunday of Advent, and the theme is Love. What is love? How can we recognize it? What does it look like? What does love feel like?

My daughter and I have this thing we do. I will say to her, "India, Mama loves you." She'll say, "I know, Mama." Then I'll say, "But do you really know? I mean, can you feel it? Do you feel my love?" She'll respond, "Yes, Mama, I feel it."

What good is it to say you love someone and they don't feel it? What's the point if those we love can't point to any evidence or practical application of that love?

In our preaching passage, I see love. And there are three characteristics that help me understand that what I see in this passage is indeed love. First, love has a Story. Second, love has a Challenge. And, finally, love has Courage.

Betrothal

Tonight, the focus of this sermon is not on Mary, but Joseph. Joseph, a young man who made a commitment to Mary, a young girl, and her family. Joseph and Mary were betrothed. In those days, a betrothal was serious business. When I say business, that is exactly what I mean. Money and property were exchanged. Joseph paid what was called "the bride-price"[44] to Mary's father. Typically, in those days, marriage was transactional. Love was not factored into the equation. Love had nothing to do with the arrangement. But this story isn't like other stories of betrothal in marriage. This one is different.

The author of life is involved in this story.

The Divine Creator's hands are all over this story.

Listen, if you want your story to be different, make sure God is involved in your story.

Before Joseph and Mary came together sexually, Joseph discovered what no person wants to find out. His partner was pregnant, and the child wasn't his! Joseph thought that someone else had been sleeping in his bed. Their story had taken a detour. Their story was presented with a challenge.

Joseph's Challenge

If you want to know if your relationship story has a chance, pay attention to how you handle challenges—setbacks, disappointments, problems, and obstacles.

Joseph had a challenge. What was he going to do? As I thought about Joseph's challenge, I couldn't help but ponder a few questions. First, what is it like to be a man who loves a woman called to special ministry by God? Well, it would mean Joseph had to adjust his life, modify his plans, and possibly take heat from his homeboys. What does it mean for a man to marry a woman who is already pregnant? A woman pregnant with a vision. Pregnant with a call. Pregnant with something inside of her placed there by God. Then I realized this is precisely what it means for a man to be the head—a phrase so often used to subjugate women to inferior status. But Joseph modeled something else. Joseph shows us that for a man to be the head, he brings out the best of his partner. Why, because the head knows his wife—sexually and otherwise—he knows her needs, he knows her potential, he knows her gifts, he knows how she's wired.

44. Wilson, "Were Mary and Joseph Married," para. 6.

Brothers, here's a word for you: You need to ask the woman you say you love, what has God placed in her that will transform the world and how can you love her so as to help her fulfill that purpose?

Joseph's Decision

The Bible says "*he decided* to call off their engagement quietly." Why, quietly, because "he didn't want to humiliate her" (Matthew 1:19).

Joseph refused to put Mary on Blast. He wasn't the man to put her seeming infidelity on Facebook, Twitter, or Instagram.

Joseph wasn't Ray Jay.

Joseph wasn't Lil Fiz.

Joseph, the Bible says, "was a righteous man" (1:19).

Evidence of his righteousness was that there were some things Joseph just wouldn't do.

Joseph wouldn't shame Mary.

Joseph wouldn't demean Mary.

Joseph wouldn't suggest that Mary might be going to hell for what he thought she had done.

Joseph was a righteous man.

And because he was righteous, he would not humiliate her. Instead, he decided to divorce her quietly.

But, how many of you know, we make our plans but God directs our steps? Joseph decided to put her away, but Joseph forgot to check in with God.

You see, God had decided too. God had something to say that would derail Joseph's decision.

"Joseph . . . don't be afraid to take Mary as your wife" (1:20), said the angel. Beloved, I was struck by the angel's word choice. Don't be "afraid."

Why would Joseph be *afraid* to marry Mary?

Reluctant, sure.

Apprehensive, OK.

Unwilling, Hesitant, and Resistant. Certainly.

But afraid. Why? Well, here it is.

Prosecute Her

According to Roman law, if a man divorced his wife, he had to do it publicly with witnesses present. He then had to bring a prosecution against her within sixty days of the divorce. If found guilty of adultery, the wife and her lover were banished to different islands for life.[45] Now, if the husband chose not to divorce her, she was immune from prosecution. But check this out; a member of the community could prosecute the husband. Caesar Augustus enacted this law somewhere between 19 to 18 BC, primarily to "increase the birthrate through encouraging marriage and stable family life."[46]

Joseph was afraid that if anyone found out Mary was pregnant by another man, and he didn't divorce her, that someone from the community would bring a case against him. The angel knew it. God knew it. Joseph didn't want to catch a case. And yet, he still decided to put Mary away quietly. Joseph took a risk.

Believe the Unbelievable

Joseph listened to the vessel sent by God. Joseph obeyed the word of God. Joseph believed the unbelievable. God calls us to the unbelievable. And when it happens, we often hesitate and vacillate wondering if God is really serious. I wonder, what is the unbelievable God is steering you to this Advent season? Enroll in seminary? Start a business? Plant a church? Quit a toxic job without another one to replace it? Who is God calling us to love? Who is God inviting us to show mercy and kindness to? Who is God calling us to hold accountable? Are you listening to God? Will you obey? Joseph obeyed God in the unbelievable. Joseph didn't understand it. He couldn't prove it. He had no witnesses to verify it. All Joseph had was the angel's word from God. And he had the willingness to believe that word and the courage to obey. Beloved, it takes courage to love. Imagine what Joseph was up against. Whoever heard of such a thing—"pregnant by the Holy Ghost! Seriously man." It takes courage to do something that's never been done before. It takes courage to obey the word God has given to only you. People will think you're irrational and foolish. I bet that's just a small portion of what Joseph dealt with. But, Joseph was a righteous man. Joseph loved. He loved God and he loved Mary.

45. Ferguson, *Backgrounds of Early Christianity*, 76.

46. Ferguson, *Backgrounds of Early Christianity*, 75.

Joseph's Love

Beloved, when a man loves a woman, he'll "give up all his comforts and sleep out in the rain."[47] When a man loves a woman, he'll bring out the best in her. When a man loves a woman, he gives her the benefit of the doubt.

Joseph loved God, and he loved Mary the way she needed to be loved. Mary, pregnant with the unbelievable, needed security. Love feels like security. Mary's womb meant danger to Empire. She needed safety. Love feels like safety. Mary, a teenage girl carrying a miracle in her body, needed acceptance and not rejection from her betrothed. Love feels like acceptance.

Beloved, I'm grateful this Advent season for this story that shows us what it looks like *when a man loves a woman*. May we learn from Joseph's love for Mary how to better love one another.

Tag-Team Sermons

The Gathering co-pastors often do what they call "tag-team" preaching, both delivering short sermons, one after another. Tag-team preaching illustrates their equal partnership, providing a model for an egalitarian community. On the first anniversary of The Gathering they preached the two sermons that follow, each titled "Why Womanist? Why Now?" but from different biblical passages.

Why Womanist? Why Now? (2 Chronicles 34:21–22)

Rev. Kamilah Hall Sharp

It is nothing short of amazing to me that today we are celebrating one year of ministry here at The Gathering. I'm excited that each of you came out to join us. I'm amazed that week after week people continue to show up and people tune in online. I'm amazed, but I probably shouldn't be. When we agreed to start a worship service here, we wanted to create space where people could come together and worship and hear womanist preaching; that has turned into The Gathering, A Womanist Church in Dallas. There are already a lot of churches in Dallas: Why Womanist? Why Now? I believe this passage helps answer these questions.

47. Lewis and Wright, "When a Man Loves a Woman," para. 2.

Here in the passage we find Josiah, the young king, trying to get things in order, especially in the house of God when Hilkiah found the book of the law. The people had been through some things, some moves, wars, hurt, and the book hadn't been seen in a long time. So, they were not sure what to do with the book. They needed counsel on how to move forward. You see the king, the priest, and all the male governmental officials couldn't figure this out, so they had to go where they could get the help they needed. They had to go to a woman, the prophet Huldah.

Though this occurred in the eighteenth year when King Josiah reigned, it sounds familiar to me now. Here in 2018 in these all but United States, when ignorance is at an all-time high, the numbers are down in the stock market and the church, it seems that now folks want to hear from women. It is not lost on me the number of women now being sought out for leadership roles, particularly Black women in corporations, academy, and the church. They are often asked for their help and leadership when things aren't going well. When everything was fine, the men could handle it—we don't need your help, ladies—but now when folks figure they have more questions than answers, more problems than solutions, we need help, so it's time to get a woman for the job.

So, Josiah and the rest of the boys decide to get Huldah, but why Huldah? Josiah could have sent for Jeremiah; he was around, but they went and got Huldah. Well, the text tells us Huldah was the royal prophet. She probably had a reputation of being trustworthy, one whose word you can depend on. Remember Jeremiah said stuff about a lot of other prophets, calling them false prophets, but we never hear him talking bad about Huldah. Huldah was one you could trust. When folks are in trouble or when they need help, they want someone they can trust. #Trustwomanists.

I believe Huldah had some experiences that were not like the men who came seeking her help. Yes, she was a prophet, but she was a woman prophet. To be clear, she wasn't the only woman prophet. Although the books of prophets all have male names, there were women prophets. But as a woman prophet, I believe there were some things she had seen, heard, and experienced as a woman living in a society filled with what we now call PMS—patriarchy, misogyny, and sexism. Huldah had some insight. She could see some things that the men did not and sometimes could not see and had some experiences with God her male counterparts did not have.

I get that as Black women in this country, there are some things we've experienced that no man has ever had to endure, no matter their race.

There are things that Black women endure that other women do not, and that is where womanism begins, but it is not where it ends. See, people will say it's just about women or just about Black women, and that's not true. Womanism is centered in the life experiences of Black women, but womanists are committed to the survival of all people. That's right, ALL people. In that commitment we recognize that living at the intersection of racism, sexism, and classism our entire lives gives us experiences that allow us to often see things others can't. We have conversations with God that others don't. The issue is that for so long there have been those who want to reject our experiences as if our truth is a lie.

There has been a constant struggle for people to believe the experiences of women are valid and have worth. As Sofia said, "All my life I had to fight!"[48] We live in a society where a woman can be forced to relive her assault in front of the world and not receive any justice. Well, I believe her and the millions of women around this world who tell their truth. Let's be honest; there are men and nonbinary people whose experiences have been ignored as well. Let me say today whatever your experience is, it is your truth, it is real and has value and no speech or tweet gone change that. I believe you and we believe womanists.

Apparently, they trusted and believed Huldah. I'm sure she still had to deal with some men who didn't support her, some who thought she shouldn't be the one speaking for God. And I'm sure it wasn't just men, but probably women too. See, womanists can relate because there are plenty of men who say, "I don't buy into all that womanist stuff or I don't believe women should be preaching." And it's not just the men; there are plenty of women on that same wagon. They don't like womanists or feminists because they are "for-men-ist." Oh, it's just like it sounds, "for-men-ism"; it's like "masculinism" in that it subscribes to the belief in the inherent superiority of men over women, but it is not developed and sustained by men but by women. We have a lot of "for-men-ists," especially in the church. And many "for-men-ists" love to quote certain Bible verses, but here's the thing: Huldah was the first person recorded in the Bible who was asked to interpret what we now call the Bible. The men brought the book of laws to her to determine if this is in fact the word of God.

I get it though, because so many times we hear people do strange things, claiming it is the word of God. Folks take the errors of their heart and mind and wrap them in the word of God. We hear people condemn

48. Walker, *The Color Purple*, 40.

the LGBTQ community in the name of God, saying politics don't belong in the church. Then a well-known Black woman Christian writer with a large platform said she does not identify herself as a Black woman. Well, when I look at the book and look at my experience with God, I don't believe any of that to be the word of God.

You see it was Huldah who had to tell them that this is the word of God. Sometimes you need a woman to give you a word from God. But to be clear, not just any woman but one who is concerned about the people and not just their pockets. Those are the ones you can trust, believe, and listen to. Trust, believe, and listen to the womanists because at this moment in time when people are being shot in grocery stores, bombs sent through the mail, and attacks on synagogues, God is still speaking. We say "how long," and yet God speaks. God still has a word of liberation, a word of hope, a word of love for you, and those words are coming through the bodies of womanists. God has been speaking through women throughout time. God spoke through Huldah, God spoke through Mary Magdalene, and God is still speaking. Are we listening?

Why Womanist? Why Now? (2 Chronicles 34:31–33)

Rev. Dr. Irie Lynne Session

The prophet Huldah is consulted about the contents of a newly found scroll in the Temple. She interprets it and confirms that God will indeed bring disaster on the house of Judah because of their idolatry and for abandoning the ways of God.

Experience of Sankofa

Huldah's interpretation of the words of the book newly found in the Temple and her affirmation of their certainty in coming to pass led King Josiah to an experience of *Sankofa*, which he instilled in the people of Jerusalem and Benjamin. *Sankofa* is an African word from the Akan tribe in Ghana. The literal translation of the word and the symbol is "it is not taboo to fetch what is at risk of being left behind." The *Sankofa* symbolizes the Akan people's quest for knowledge—through critical examination, and intelligent and patient investigation. The symbol is based on a mythical bird with its feet firmly planted forward with its head turned backwards. Thus, the Akan believe the past serves as a guide for planning the future. To the Akan, it is this wisdom in learning from the past that ensures a strong future. *Sankofa* calls on us to look back and glean wisdom from the ancestors in order to move into a better future. The prophet Huldah inquired of God and interpreted the words of the book in a way that caused King Josiah to look back—to reflect on their ancestors.

Ancestors

Use of the word "ancestors," particularly in verses 32–33, brought to mind a lecture presented by Rev. Dr. Frank Thomas a couple weeks ago during Scholars Week at Memphis Theological Seminary. In his lecture, Dr. Thomas discussed gaining wisdom from the ancestors, or what he called "Wisdom of the Ages." For many Black people, ancestors serve as our guides and wisdom bearers. We believe that through prayer, connecting with older members of our families, and retelling the stories of our ancestors, surviving and thriving against the odds, we as Black folk always have access to that wisdom. As womanists, we look to ancestral stories to help us strategize ways to move forward as pastoral leaders, as preachers, as theologians, heck, as Black women, in spite of the racist and sexist obstacles we face every single day. And, from reading this text, it's obvious to me that God also takes seriously the stories of the ancestors.

In the case of Judah, God is set to bring judgment on them because of the unrighteousness and the injustice of their ancestors. Because they "did not keep the word of the LORD, to act in accordance with all that was written in this book" (2 Chronicles 34:21). Disobedience and lack of concern for the word of the LORD became a lifestyle that was passed down through the generations. Certain of their ancestors were not persuaded that it was in their best interest to keep the word of the LORD.

Unpersuadable

Two weeks ago, Rev. Kamilah and I along with a few other preachers discussed this very idea. One of the pastors, a professor in Memphis, helped us see that some people are just not persuadable. They have believed, bought into, and benefited from living in opposition to the good purposes of God for so many generations that they are now unpersuadable. There are people we will never convince of the reality of white supremacy and its death-dealing effects in church or society. Some will never open their eyes wide enough or see that racism is in the DNA of America. And still others will resist any biblical translation other than the King James Version. The faith, religious ideologies, and practices of our ancestors make their way into our lives—even when we think they haven't. Which is why I believe some folk want to disengage themselves from the actions of their ancestors and while others of us are eager to learn more about the courage and strength of ours. Which is one of the reasons this text appeals to me.

Huldah, in a critical time in the life of Judah, was called upon as one with religious authority who had the ear of God and the ability to interpret the words of the book. One who could possibly assuage God's anger and ameliorate the consequences of the disobedience of their ancestors. To be sure, there were two other prophets during the reign of King Josiah who could have been consulted, Zephaniah and Jeremiah. However, the priest went to the prophet Huldah.

But why Huldah?

Wil Gafney, in her book *Daughters of Miriam: Women Prophets in Ancient Israel*, says of Huldah, "She is the prophetic authority behind the reform usually attributed to King Josiah of Judah."[49] Perhaps Huldah had a way of communicating prophecy that was more conducive to delivering news difficult to hear. I don't know; maybe as a woman prophet Huldah had a certain kind of wisdom born from experiencing the difficulties of prophetic ministry. Although there were other women prophets, they were still in the minority. What I think is most important is not why the prophet Huldah was consulted, but that she was the go-to prophet in a critical moment in Judah's history. And, that her voice was heard and she was believed.

Womanist Wisdom

What would it look like if Black women's voices were heard and believed? I use Black women in a general sense, understanding that Black women are not monolithic—we do not all think the same, act the same, believe the same, or theologize the same. So, generally speaking, what would it look like if the prophetic utterances of Black preaching women and their ways of interpreting the biblical text were taken seriously rather than marginalized? What if the church, the academy, and larger society *made central Black women's ways of knowing?*

49. Gafney, *Daughters of Miriam*, 96.

You see, Black women have what scholars call an "epistemological advantage"; an "epistemological advantage" describes the ways in which Black women are able to have a much clearer understanding of how power structure works within a given society because we are not members of the dominant group. As women living at the intersections of race, class, and gender oppression, Black women have knowledge of the practices of our contexts as well as those of the dominant culture. Another way of expressing this way of knowing is *Womanist Wisdom.*

Linda Hollies, in her book *Bodacious Womanist Wisdom*, writes, "Womanist Wisdom is that learned by Black women who have grappled with issues of race, sex, and class discrimination and yet continue to rise above the odds and the world's expectations. Womanist Wisdom gives you a word of knowledge. It's not the easy way. But it's the way of courage."[50]

Churches, nonprofits, businesses, schools, colleges, universities, and seminaries who fail to make central the voices and perspectives of Black women in their employ are missing out on a critical mass of knowledge and expertise that could catapult their organizations to another stratosphere. Because we really do have that Magic.

Melissa Harris-Perry, in her book *Sister Citizen: Shame, Stereotypes, and Black Women in America*, writes of womanist wisdom in terms of Black women as the canaries in the coal mines of society.[51] "To be a 'canary in a coal mine' means that one is so sensitive to environmental conditions that one's suffering sends a warning signal to others nearby. This expression comes from the practice of using canaries as alarms in mining tunnels. The canary's lungs are so delicate that they are affected by the toxic gases and die."[52] It's dangerous being a canary. Womanists have determined to be more than canaries in the coal mines of the church and the academy. We're tired of dying trying to get the church to see the toxic fumes of white supremacy, patriarchy, sexism, and racism. And so, we create, we innovate, and with God's help, we make room for ourselves. We build our own tables where we can live into the fullness of who God made us to be, women who care about and are actively engaged in work and ministry leading to the survival and wholeness of entire peoples, male and female.

So, Why Womanist? Because when we look back, we see that the playing field has never been level for us.

50. Hollies, *Bodacious Womanist Wisdom*, x.

51. Harris-Perry, *Sister Citizen*, 16.

52. Simpson, "Black Women Must Be More," para. 1.

Why Womanist? Because when we look back, we're reminded that Black women have always been treated as objects, rarely as subjects.

Why Womanist? Because when we look back, it's clear to us that the Black woman is and has always been the most disrespected woman on the planet.

Why Womanist? Why Now? Because we will get the RESPECT we deserve or we'll leave the table—wherever it is.

Why Womanist? Why Now? Because when we look back, we remember that God has fortified us with the strength, the tenacity, the internal equipment, and the ancestral legacy to Still Rise.

Why Womanist? Why Now? Because the church, the academy, and the larger society need Huldahs who have the ear of God. We need Huldahs who can interpret the words in the BOOK in a manner that elicits a resistance to every power and principality that keeps us from becoming the beloved community.

Why Womanist? Why Now? Well, why not?

5

Litanies for a Womanist Church

WOMANIST WORSHIP MOVES THEOLOGY and biblical interpretation from the head to the heart. Invigorating not only the mind, womanist worship also converts the imagination and empowers social justice activism. Womanist worship shapes values, stirs spirits, and drives actions. Along with sermons, litanies and music and all parts of a worship service are vital to womanist worship. This chapter includes litanies created for The Gathering, a Womanist Church. Included in the worship services of The Gathering, these litanies contribute to the liberating, transformative mission of this unique womanist church.

Together, Changing the World

ONE: Come, let us worship our Mother and Father, the Ground of our being, the Source of our lives, the Spirit who sets us free.

ALL: We come together to celebrate our partnership as sisters and brothers in ministry to transform our lives and to create an equitable world.

ONE: We gather to share one another's burdens and blessings, trials and triumphs.

ALL: As partners with Jesus and with one another, we bring healing and hope to our wounded world.

ONE: The Spirit calls us to wholehearted commitment to our mission of dismantling patriarchy, racism, and all injustices.

ALL: We move forward together side by side, empowered by the Spirit.

ONE: Our mission of inclusiveness is not easy in our time and place. Let us dare to believe that we contribute to healing our global community by gathering here as a faith community to share our visions of transformation.

ALL: Let us dare to dream big dreams of bringing justice and peace to our community and our world.

ONE: All voices and all gifts are vital to make our dreams reality.

ALL: Together, we change the world.

Faith Becoming Reality

ONE: We come together to profess our faith, our assurance of things hoped for, of things not seen.

ALL: We gather with open minds and spirits, believing we will receive new revelations.

ONE: Our worship is an act of faith in the Spirit of Love alive in each of us.

ALL: We speak and sing our visions as we reclaim our wholeness, our power in the image of the Divine.

ONE: Here at The Gathering we breathe the air of a time yet to be, a time when barriers are broken down and wounds are healed.

ALL: The Spirit gives us visions of what can be, guiding us forward to more than we can see.

ONE: Our faith becomes reality as we work so that all can be free.

ALL: Let us worship with hope and faith that
silenced voices will be heard,
trembling voices will be made strong,
oppressed people will be set free,
by power of the Spirit within us
at work yesterday, today, and forever.

Open to Epiphany

ONE: We gather here with hearts and minds open to Epiphany, to new revelations.

ALL: Revelations of the Divine did not stop with the Magi and the woman at the well.

ONE: Epiphany continues to happen where minds and souls are open.

ALL: We open ourselves to new revelations of divinity within, among, and above us.

ONE: The news these days reveals a world longing for Epiphany. Children are suffering and dying from abuse, violence, exploitation, and poverty. Women, men, and children suffer oppression and discrimination because of race, gender, class, and religion.

ALL: We pray and work together for a world open to divine revelations, as the Magi and the woman at the well were open to revelations of the Messiah.

ONE: Epiphany beckons us forward to satisfy our longing and the world's longing for new life.

ALL: We stand together on tiptoe, breathless for new discovery.

Partners in Transforming Our World

ONE: Loving Mother-Father Creator, Liberating Jesus, Empowering Spirit, we gather here to worship you and to call on you for renewed strength.

ALL: Give us a faith that will not shrink though we are pressed and distressed. Give us a faith that sustains us through every storm and alarm.

ONE: We claim your promise that when we hope in you, we will "renew our strength"; we will "mount up with wings like eagles"; we will "run and not be weary"; we will "walk and not faint" (Isaiah 40:31).

ALL: Your "perfect love casts out fear" (1 John 4:18). By faith we receive your love and let go of fear.

ONE: We marvel that you have created each one of us in your divine image with creative potential beyond our imagining.

ALL: Guide us to deeper discovery of our creativity, our passion, our calling.

ONE: Calm our doubts and fears with memories of past times of exhilaration in the flow of your creative energy, doing what we're created to do.

ALL: Hold us near, and free us from fear, as we claim all our gifts and dream big.

ONE: Give us a faith that never gives up, that keeps moving us forward to fulfill our passions and dreams of making a difference in the world.

ALL: Empower us to become all we're meant to be as individuals and as a faith community. By faith we claim your divine image and partner with you in transforming our world.

Making All Things New

ONE: We gather in the power of the Holy Spirit. She is making all things new!

ALL: The Holy Spirit pours out Her gifts on all of us. We celebrate the rainbow of gifts in our community, enhancing our ministry together.

ONE: We do not invest our gifts in possessions or store up treasures for ourselves. We believe Jesus that "life does not consist in the abundance of possessions" (Luke 12:15).

ALL: The Holy Spirit guides us to invest our gifts in making a difference in the lives of others. We invest in loving others and ourselves. We bring our gifts together to create a more loving and just church and society.

ONE: The Loving Spirit empowers us to go out together on our mission of dismantling racism, patriarchy, misogyny, sexism, and other intersecting injustices.

ALL: As partners we claim the Holy Spirit's power for this big mission, and we join with Her to set the oppressed free.

ONE: The Life-Giving Spirit stirs our visions of new creation. She gives us visions of a world where all are free to become all we are created to be in the divine image.

ALL: We join our gifts to make our visions reality by the power of the Holy Spirit. We dare to believe that She and we together are making all things new!

Celebrating All Creation

ONE: We gather here to praise our Loving Creator, who made all of us good and whole in the divine image. We praise our Gracious Redeemer who came not to condemn but to bring healing and abundant life. We praise the Life-Giving Spirit who lives and moves in all of us.

ALL: Come, let us celebrate, for we are wonderfully made!

ONE: Praise the Source of all creation, giving life throughout the earth,
blessing every love relation, filling all with sacred worth.

ALL: Celebrate all forms and colors, varied beauty everywhere,
streams of goodness overflowing, wondrous gifts for all to share.

ONE: Many genders, many races, all reflect Divinity;
many gifts and many graces help us be all we can be.

ALL: Partners on this path of freedom, taking down each stifling wall,
we will open doors of welcome, bringing hope and joy to all.

ONE: Long have many been excluded, judged and scorned by custom's norms; everyone will be included as we work to make reforms.

ALL: Let us end abuse and violence, bringing justice everywhere,
joining Holy Wisdom's mission, helping all be free and fair.

ONE: Equal relationships free and nurture body, mind, and soul, reaffirming every person, all created good and whole.

ALL: Come, rejoice and join together, celebrating life and love; praise the great Creative Spirit, living in us and above.[1]

Litany of Lament

ONE: In the U.S. alone, every 9 seconds a woman is battered.[2]

ALL: We lament this violence, and cry out for it to stop.

ONE: In the U.S. alone, women experience an estimated 4.8 million partner-related physical assaults and rapes every year.[3]

ALL: We lament this violence, and cry out for it to stop.

ONE: Every day in the U.S., more than three women are murdered by their husbands or boyfriends.[4] Black women are almost three times as likely as white women to die from domestic violence.[5]

ALL: We lament this violence, and cry out for it to stop.

ONE: One in three women in the world experiences some kind of abuse in her lifetime.[6]

ALL: We lament this violence, and cry out for it to stop.

ONE: We all share the pain of violence. Church and society have often silenced us, conditioning us to feel responsible for the violence inflicted upon us. We have suffered from unhealthy theological views about responding to violence.

ALL: Growing up in patriarchal churches and cultures, we have all suffered abuse and injustice.

ONE: Wisdom cries out; she raises Her voice, "How long, how long will scoffers delight in their scoffing?" (Proverbs 1:22). Jesus

1. Aldredge-Clanton, "Praise the Source of All Creation," 28–29.
2. "Every 9 Seconds in the US," para 5.
3. "Pledge to End Violence Against Women."
4. Jeltson, "3 Women Are Killed Every Day," para 1–2.
5. Jones, "Why Black Women Struggle," para. 4.
6. "Violence Against Women," para. 2.

cries out, "Forgive them; for they do not know what they are doing" (Luke 23:34).

ALL: We cry out with Wisdom, who has been scoffed and abused. We cry out with Jesus, who suffered violence and scorn.

ONE: Wisdom shows us how to follow Jesus in forgiving, not as excusing or silencing or rushing past our feelings. We forgive so that experiences of violence no longer control or limit us.

ALL: Forgiveness frees us to claim abundant life and all we're created to be in the divine image.

Litany for Cyntoia Brown[7] #freecyntoiabrownprayerofconfession

ONE: Mercy-filled God who loves and cares about the widow, the orphan, the stranger—those who are most vulnerable—you are tenderhearted toward those who have been abandoned, mistreated, and oppressed.

ALL: We confess that our hearts have been hard.

ONE: God, despite your mercy toward us, we have hidden ourselves from the most vulnerable in society. Our fear of knowing, seeing, and responding appropriately to victims has exacerbated their suffering.

ALL: We confess our culpability in the suffering of Cyntoia Brown and all of her sisters.

ONE: Our collective ignorance of the trauma experienced by victims of sex trafficking, commercial sexual exploitation, domestic violence, and sexual abuse has inhibited us from engaging the systemic evils that oppress women and girls.

ALL: We confess our willful ignorance.

7. Cyntoia Brown, a victim of sex trafficking, served fifteen years of a life sentence for killing a man who raped her when she was sixteen. The Gathering's ministry partners joined others in writing letters to the governor for clemency. Tennessee Governor Bill Haslam granted clemency in 2019, and she was released from prison.

ONE: Our fear of meaningful and authentic engagement with those who suffer sexual violence, sexual abuse, and sex trafficking has caused us to be apathetic to the plight of Cyntoia Brown and all her sisters.

ALL: We confess our fear and apathy,

ONE: Creator God, although you created female and male in your own image to work in partnership, we your people have created a world that denigrates and subordinates women and girls. Young women like Cyntoia Brown and her sisters.

ALL: We confess our internalized, covert, and overt sexism and gender bias.

ONE: God of all nations, tribes, and peoples, we've done a poor job of dismantling the racism in our own hearts and within the larger society. Our implicit biases allowed jurors to convict a 16-year-old Cyntoia Brown, a survivor of rape, sexual assault, and violence, to life in prison for shooting the man who raped her.

ALL: We confess our racism and implicit bias.

ALL: God, hear our prayer of confession. And may our fruit bear witness that our hearts are being transformed.

Reshaped

ONE: Patriarchy and racism have misshaped relationships between Black women and white women. Fear, distrust, and competition have blocked our connections.

ALL: The Potter continually reshapes us. She brings women of diverse races together to dismantle patriarchy and to create an equitable world.

ONE: Ruth and Naomi transcended ethnic prejudices to join together for their own survival and the survival of others in a patriarchal society.

ALL: The Potter continually shapes and reshapes us. She brings women of different cultures together to resist patriarchal oppression and to work for the survival and wholeness of all people.

ONE: White women in the suffrage movement excluded Black women because they feared their cause would be hindered. But when Sojourner Truth delivered her famous "Ain't I a Woman" speech, they realized the power of Black and white women's collaboration. Frances Gage wrote, "Sojourner had taken us up in her strong arms and carried us safely over the slough of difficulty, turning the whole tide in our favor."[8]

ALL: The Potter continually reshapes us. She brings Black women and white women together in resistance to patriarchy.

ONE: In spite of opposition and danger, Black women and white women collaborated in the Civil Rights Movement. Rev. Dr. Prathia Hall and Joyce Barrett resisted racism and sexism as they worked together on the Student Nonviolent Coordinating Committee.[9]

ALL: The Potter continually shapes and reshapes us. She brings Black women and white women together to free people from racial and gender injustices.

ONE: Womanist Alice Walker and feminist Gloria Steinem collaborated on *Ms. Magazine*, serving as co-editors.

ALL: The Potter continually shapes us. She brings Black women and white women together in creative work for social justice.

ONE: The Potter is shaping and reshaping us here at The Gathering. In this time and place She is bringing a beautiful mosaic of races and genders together to dismantle racism, patriarchy, sexism, and misogyny, so all can thrive.

ALL: Together we are beautiful. Together we are genius. All together we have power!

8. Gage, "Ain't I a Woman? Sojourner Truth via Frances Gage," para. 6.
9. Pace, *Freedom Faith*, 66–67.

Celebrating the Second Anniversary of The Gathering

ONE: We come together to celebrate The Gathering: A Womanist Church, birthed two years ago by visionary ministers in partnership with our Mother-Father Creator.

ALL: We celebrate The Gathering, where all are truly welcome and where we partner in ministry to transform our lives and to go out to create an equitable world.

ONE: We gather to celebrate two years of Womanist God-talk, calling us into a community of justice in partnership with a liberating Jesus.

ALL: As partners in The Gathering, we move forward in faith into a future of transformative ministry.

ONE: The Holy Spirit calls us to wholehearted commitment to our mission of dismantling racism, patriarchy, misogyny, sexism, and other intersecting injustices.

ALL: Together we work for gender, racial, and LGBTQIA equality, empowered by the Spirit.

ONE: Our equity mission is not easy in our time and place.

ALL: Together we resist all injustices and persist in demanding equity, justice, and peace. We persist until we get a Yes!

ONE: Let us dare to believe that our Mother-Father Creator will give us all that we need to fulfill our mission. We persist in asking until we get a Yes!

ALL: All together we have power, rising up against all the wrong;
all together we have power, rising up to sing freedom songs.[10]
All together, we are changing the world!

Speak Out

ONE: "Speak out for those who cannot speak, for the rights of all the destitute. Speak out, judge righteously, defend the rights of the poor and needy" (Proverbs 31:8–9).

10. Aldredge-Clanton, "All Together," 20–21.

ALL: In The Gathering community we find courage and power to speak out for all those who are oppressed.

ONE: "Injustice anywhere is a threat to justice everywhere."[11]

ALL: If we do nothing when we see people suffering from sexism, racism, heterosexism, classism, and other injustices, we threaten justice for everyone.

ONE: When we speak out against injustices, we all experience healing. When we break the bonds of injustice, healing springs up everywhere.

ALL: When we share with the poor and hungry, we create a better world for everyone.

ONE: Sister-Brother Spirit at work within this community gives us power to free ourselves and others from oppression.

ALL: Together we worship and work to dismantle patriarchy and white supremacy at the root of systemic injustices.

ONE: Now our light breaks "forth like the dawn," and our "healing" springs "up quickly" (Isaiah 58:8).

ALL: Now we are transforming our lives together, creating a just and peaceful world.

Choose Life

ONE: We gather here to follow the ways of Divine Wisdom. We choose life.

ALL: When we partner in ministry to transform our lives and to create an equitable world through The Gathering, we choose life.

ONE: We gather as partners to follow Divine Wisdom within and among us. "Her ways are ways of pleasantness, and all Her paths are" justice and "peace"(Proverbs 3:17).

ALL: When we follow Her paths of justice and peace, we choose life.

ONE: Divine Wisdom guides and empowers us to work together to dismantle systemic structures that oppress people.

11. King, "Letter from Birmingham Jail," 77.

ALL: When we dismantle racism, patriarchy, misogyny, sexism, and other systemic injustices, we choose life.

ONE: Divine Wisdom empowers us to work together for racial, gender, and LGBTQIA equity.

ALL: When we work for racial, gender, and LGBTQIA equity, we choose life.

ONE: Divine Wisdom guides us to share our material resources and to work for economic justice so that no one suffers from poverty and hunger.

ALL: When we share our resources and work for economic justice, we choose life.

ONE: Divine Wisdom empowers us to care for all creation, to conserve and nurture the beauty of creation.

ALL: When we care for all creation, we choose life.

ONE: Divine Wisdom guides us to choose words and actions that bless not curse, heal not harm.

ALL: When our words and actions bless and heal, we choose life.

ONE: Divine Wisdom is a "tree of life," and those who follow Her receive blessings. (Proverbs 3:18)

ALL: When we follow Divine Wisdom, we choose life and blessings.

ONE: Blessed are those who follow Divine Wisdom. "For Her income is better than silver, and Her revenue better than gold. She is more precious than jewels, and nothing you desire can compare with her" (Proverbs 3:14–15).

ALL: As partners we follow the just and peaceful ways of Divine Wisdom. We choose life. Now we can feel grace-drops falling on us. Showers of blessings are coming!

Proclaiming Big Dreams

ONE: Come, let us proclaim our faith in the Creator of all life,
the Solid Rock on whom we stand,
the Spirit who stirs visions within us.

ALL: Together we celebrate our faith and encourage one another to keep our faith strong, steady, and growing.

ONE: In this community we find faith to endure
struggles and sufferings, fears and frustrations.
We stand together on the Solid Rock,
who gives us courage and strength.

ALL: As partners with one another and with all who suffer,
we work to end abuses and injustices.
By faith we move forward together on our mission of
dismantling racism, patriarchy, misogyny, and sexism.

ONE: Together we draw power from the Spirit, who supports our justice call and takes down every wall. On Her we can depend; Her grace and goodness never end.

ALL: The desires of our hearts are placed by the Spirit. She gives us all that we need to make our dreams reality.

ONE: So let us claim and proclaim our big dreams, moving forward with steadfast faith.

ALL: We envision a world of loving kindness, justice, peace, and equity, a world where people of all races, genders, and cultures are free to become all we are created to be in the divine image.
If our vision seems delayed, we will "wait for it." We will live by faith, believing that "it will surely come" (Habakkuk 2:3).

About the Contributors

Diana T. Clark is Executive Director of Youth Conflict Resolution Center in Dallas, Texas. She founded the Center because of her concern for youth in the community. Diana received the 2019 City of Dallas Park and Recreation Community Partner Award. Born during the civil rights era, she completed high school and a Bachelor of Social Work degree in St. Louis, Missouri. Her Christian journey began with her family in the African Methodist Episcopal Church and continues with The Gathering.

Nommo Kofi Diop is an artist who combines social justice themes with visions of possibilities. Over forty years he has painted and sketched, creating a style of art to describe his external and internal worlds. His artwork is influenced by his experiences of racism, study of the history of forced brutality suffered by African people, and feelings of connection with his African people. Nommo has a Bachelor of Arts degree from San Jose State University in California.

Olivia Catherine Gray moved from the Washington, DC, area to Dallas to become project manager of the first Shark Tank project to bring economic development to the South Dallas community. She worked over thirty years as a respiratory therapist and has worked as a real estate agent. She has a Bachelor of Science degree in Criminal Justice and is currently applying to Brite Divinity School. Olivia enjoys traveling in Europe, quilting, listening to music, playing card games, and Sudoku.

Rev. Winner A. Laws is a womanist pastor, spiritually called to let **ALL** people (Black, LGBTQIA, American Indian, Hispanic) know that God loves them unconditionally. She serves as the Congregational Care and Spiritual Support Minister at The Gathering, A Womanist Church in Dallas, Texas. She has a Bachelor of Science degree from Carnegie Mellon University and a Master of Theological Studies degree from Brite Divinity School at Texas Christian University. Her passions include faith development, leadership, family, and golf.

Phil Lucia has been attempting to be a Christian for all but roughly forty-eight hours of his life. In addition to his work wrangling denominations and publishing scores for Church Clarity and ministry partnership at The Gathering, he also plays music, reads voraciously, and is employed hawking gearboxes for industrial automation. You can often find him hanging out with his son and living the Millennial dream in McKinney, Texas. Follow him on Twitter at @philluciaTX.

Alexandria McLemore is from Carrollton, Texas, and is currently a volunteer coordinator and ministry partner of The Gathering. She has a BA in Literary Studies from the University of Texas at Dallas, and an MA in Multicultural Women's & Gender Studies from Texas Woman's University. Alexandria is a proud Black Feminist & Womanist, and is extremely grateful for her amazing parents, brother and his four beautiful children. She loves to read, write, watch awesome movies, and attend The Gathering.

Vontril Lilly McLemore was born in Carthage, Texas, and is currently a ministry partner of The Gathering. She's the oldest of eight children, and attended Mountain View College and Bishop College. Vontril married the love of her life in 1974, and is the proud mother of two amazing children. She also worked as a postal employee for twenty-seven years. In her spare time, she enjoys singing, cooking, meeting new people, and connecting with the badass women of The Gathering.

Rev. V. Ruth Schulenberg finished coursework and is preparing for exams for the PhD in Pastoral Theology at Brite Divinity School. She has ministerial standing in the Christian Church (Disciples of Christ) and is an ACPE Certified Educator, teaching people how to do interfaith, multicultural spiritual care at a Dallas area hospital. Since 2018, Ruth has been a ministry partner of The Gathering. Her interests include anti-racism work, end-of-life planning and care, and social justice in the healthcare setting.

Bibliography

Aldredge-Clanton, Jann. "All Together We Have Power." *Inclusive Songs for Resistance & Social Action*. Fort Worth, TX: Eakin, 2018.

———. "Praise the Source of All Creation." *Earth Transformed with Music! Inclusive Songs for Worship*. Fort Worth, TX: Eakin, 2015.

Alexander, Jeffrey C., et al. "Toward a Theory of Cultural Trauma." In *Cultural Trauma and Collective Identity*, 1–30. Berkeley: University of California Press, 2004. www.jstor.org/stable/10.1525/j.ctt1pp9nb.4.

"American Community Survey: Household Type." *U.S. Census Bureau* (2017). https://data.census.gov/cedsci/table?q=American%20Community%20Survey%3A%20Household%20Type,%20Black%20or%20African%20American%20Women%20Alone,%202017&tid=ACSDT1Y2017.B11001B&t=Black%20or%20African%20American%3AHousehold%20Size%20and%20Type&y=2017.

"American Community Survey: Selected Population Profile." *U.S. Census Bureau* (2017). https://data.census.gov/cedsci/table?q=Selected%20Population%20Profile%202017,%20Black%20or%20African%20American%20female%20headed%20households,%20poverty%20level&tid=ACSDT1Y2017.B17010B&t=Black%20or%20African%20American%3APoverty&y=2017.

Benbow, Candice. "While More Black Churches Come Online Due to Coronavirus, Black Women Faith Leaders Have Always Been Here." *Essence Magazine* (March 24, 2020). https://www.essence.com/feature/more-black-churches-online-coronavirus-black-women-faith-leaders-always-been-here/.

Browning, Elizabeth Barrett. "How Do I Love Thee? (Sonnet 43)." *Poets.org*. https://poets.org/poem/how-do-i-love-thee-sonnet-43.

Cannon, Katie Geneva. Quoted in "A Deeper Shade of Purple: 10 Essential Womanist Texts." *The Culture*. http://theculture.forharriet.com/2015/08/a-deeper-shade-of-purple-10-essential_18.html.

———. *Katie's Canon: Womanism and the Soul of the Black Community*. New York: Continuum, 1995.

Chaney, Marvin L. "Whose Sour Grapes? The Addressees of Isaiah 5:1–7 in the Light of Political Economy." *Semeia* 87 (1999) 105–22.

Coleman, Monica A., ed. *Ain't I A Womanist Too? Third-Wave Womanist Religious Thought*. Kindle ed. Minneapolis: Fortress, 2013.

———. *Making a Way Out of No Way: A Womanist Theology*. Minneapolis: Fortress, 2008.

"The Combahee River Collective Statement." *The Combahee River Collective* (1978) 1–11. https://americanstudies.yale.edu/sites/default/files/files/Keyword%20Coalition_Readings.pdf.

Copeland, M. Shawn. "Wading Through Many Sorrows: Toward a Theology of Suffering in Womanist Perspective." In *A Troubling in My Soul: Womanist Perspectives on Evil and Suffering*, edited by Emilie Townes, 109–29. Maryknoll, NY: Orbis, 2015.

Crawford, A. Elaine Brown. *Hope in the Holler: A Womanist Theology.* Louisville: Westminster John Knox, 2002.

Crenshaw, Kimberlé. "Mapping the Margins: Intersectionality, Identity Politics, and Violence Against Women of Color." *Stanford Law Review* 43/6 (1991) 1241–99.

Crenshaw, Kimberlé, et al. *Say Her Name: Resisting Police Brutality Against Black Women.* African American Policy Forum, Center for Intersectionality and Social Policy Studies. New York: Columbia Law School, 2015.

"Current Population Survey, Annual Social and Economic (ASEC) Supplement: Table PINC-05: Work Experience in 2017—People 15 Years Old and Over by Total Money Earnings in 2017, Age, Race, Hispanic Origin, Sex, and Disability Status." *U.S. Census Bureau* (2017). https://www.census.gov/data/tables/time-series/demo/income-poverty/cps-pinc/pinc-05.2017.html.

Day, Keri. *Unfinished Business: Black Women, the Black Church, and the Struggle to Thrive in America.* Maryknoll, NY: Orbis, 2012.

DiAngelo, Robin. *White Fragility: Why It's So Hard for White People to Talk About Racism.* Kindle ed. Boston: Beacon, 2018.

Douglas, Kelly Brown. *Black Bodies and the Black Church: A Blues Slant.* New York: Palgrave MacMillan, 2012.

Ellison, Ralph. *Invisible Man.* New York: Random, 1952.

"Every 9 Seconds in the US a Woman Is Assaulted or Beaten—Help End Domestic Violence." *Cision PRWeb* (Austin, TX: October 8, 2012). http://www.prweb.com/releases/2012/10/prweb9986276.htm.

Felder, Cain Hope. "Cultural Ideology, Afrocentrism, and Biblical Interpretation." In *Black Theology: A Documentary History*, edited by James H. Cone and Gayraud Gilmore, 2:184–95. 2 vols. Maryknoll, NY: Orbis, 1993.

Ferguson, Everett. *Backgrounds of Early Christianity.* 3rd ed. Grand Rapids: Eerdmans, 2003.

Flunder, Yvette. "A Womanist Ecclesiology." *YouTube* (August, 4, 2014). https://youtu.be/hH1p5Wn60XM.

Gafney, Wilda C. *Daughters of Miriam: Woman Prophets in Ancient Israel.* Minneapolis: Fortress, 2008.

———. *Womanist Midrash: A Reintroduction to the Women of the Torah and the Throne.* Louisville: Westminster John Knox, 2017.

———. "A Womanist Midrash of Delilah: Don't Hate the Playa Hate the Game." In *Womanist Interpretations of the Bible: Expanding the Discourse*, edited by Gay L. Byron and Vanessa Lovelace, 49–72. Atlanta, GA: SBL, 2016.

Gage, Frances. "Ain't I a Woman? Sojourner Truth via Frances Gage, 1881." *Women's History Guide.* https://womenshistory.info/aint-woman-sojourner-truth-via-frances-gage-1881/.

"Gathering Staff." *The Gathering, A Womanist Church.* https://www.thegatheringexperience.com/gathering-staff.html.

Gudorf, Christine E. *Body, Sex, and Pleasure: Reconstructing Christian Sexual Ethics.* Cleveland, OH: Pilgrim, 1994.

Harris, Melanie L. *Ecowomanism: African American Women and Earth-Honoring Faiths.* Maryknoll, NY: Orbis, 2017.

———. "Ecowomanism: An Introduction." *Worldviews: Global Religions, Culture, and Ecology* 20 (2016) 5–14.

Harris-Perry, Melissa. *Sister Citizen: Shame, Stereotypes, and Black Women in America.* New Haven: Yale University Press, 2013.

Hayes, Lyn Norris. *Digging Deeper Wells: Facilitating Conversation Between the Listener and the Preacher to Aid in the Practical Application of a Womanist Hermeneutic.* Unpublished Doctor of Ministry dissertation. Memphis Theological Seminary.

Haynes, Frederick D., III. "Headlights or Taillights: Examining Strategies for a Christian Response to Racialized Violence." Speech delivered at "Turning Tables Teach-In: Christian Response to Racialized Violence," Brite Divinity School, Fort Worth, TX (September 22, 2014). https://www.youtube.com/watch?time_continue=6231&v=uuuvCpjRS30&feature=emb_logo.

Hendricks, Obery M., Jr. *The Politics of Jesus: Rediscovering the True Revolutionary Nature of Jesus' Teachings and How They Have Been Corrupted.* New York: Doubleday, 2006.

Hollies, Linda H. *Bodacious Womanist Wisdom.* Cleveland, OH: Pilgrim, 2003.

hooks, bell. "bell hooks: Cultural Criticism & Transformation." *Media Education Foundation Transcript* (1997). https://www.mediaed.org/transcripts/Bell-Hooks-Transcript.pdf.

Hurston, Zora Neale. Quoted in "If You Are Silent About Your Pain, They'll Kill You and Say You Enjoyed It," by Amed Kinsley. *Grandmother: The Definitive Record of Africa* (April 30, 2015). http://grandmotherafrica.com/if-you-are-silent-about-your-pain-theyll-kill-you-and-say-you-enjoyed-it/.

Jeltsen, Melissa. "3 Women Are Killed Every Day by Their Partners. Here Are 59 Ideas on How to Stop the Violence." *Huffpost* (March 30, 2016). https://www.huffpost.com/entry/how-to-stop-domestic-violence-murder_n_56eeb745e4b09bf44a9d85f6.

Johnson, Kimberly P. *The Womanist Preacher: Proclaiming Womanist Rhetoric from the Pulpit.* Lanham, MD: Lexington, 2017.

Jones, Feminista. "Why Black Women Struggle More with Domestic Violence." *Time* (September 10, 2014). https://time.com/3313343/ray-rice-black-women-domestic-violence/.

King, Martin Luther, Jr. *The Autobiography of Martin Luther King,* Jr. New York: Warner, 1998.

———. Quoted in "Let MLK Trouble Your Conscience," by Kevin P. Considine. *U.S. Catholic: Faith in Real Life* (April 2, 2018). http://www.uscatholic.org/articles/201804/let-mlk-trouble-your-conscience-31350.

———. "Letter from Birmingham Jail." In *Why We Can't Wait.* New York: Penguin, 1964.

Lakoff, George. *Moral Politics: How Liberals and Conservatives Think.* 3rd ed. Chicago: University of Chicago Press, 2016.

Lewis, Calvin, and Andrew Wright. "When a Man Loves a Woman." *MetroLyrics.* https://www.metrolyrics.com/when-a-man-loves-a-woman-lyrics-michael-bolton.html.

Liddle, M., et al. "Trauma and Young Offenders: A Review of the Research and Practice Literature." *Beyond Youth Custody* (2016) 1–73. http://www.beyondyouthcustody.net/resources/publications/trauma-young-offenders-review-research-practice-literature/.

Lightsey, Pamela R. *Our Lives Matter: A Womanist Queer Theology*. Eugene, OR: Pickwick, 2015.

Lilly, Harold. "It's All God." *Lyrics*. https://www.lyrics.com/lyric/25257630/Various+Artists/It%27s+All+God.

Lorde, Audre. "Age, Race, Class, and Sex: Women Redefining Difference." *CUNY Academic Commons*. https://wgs10016.commons.gc.cuny.edu/lorde-age-race-class-and-sex-women-redefining-difference/.

———. "Your Silences Will Not Protect You." *Interference* (November 28, 2013). https://www.interference.cc/tag/audre-lord/.

Macon, Alex. "Dallas Ranked Dead Last in Study of Economic Inclusivity." *D Magazine* (April 26, 2018). https://www.dmagazine.com/frontburner/2018/04/dallas-ranked-dead-last-in-study-of-economic-inclusivity/.

Malcolm X. "Who Taught You to Hate Yourself?" Speech at the funeral service of Ronald Stokes in Los Angeles, May 5, 1962. *Genius*. https://genius.com/Malcolm-x-who-taught-you-to-hate-yourself-annotated.

Mandela, Nelson. Quoted in "A Selection of Quotes from the Late Nelson Mandela." *Nelson Mandela Foundation* (2020). https://www.nelsonmandela.org/content/page/a-selection-of-nelson-mandela-quotes.

McFague, Sallie. *Blessed are the Consumers: Climate Change and the Practice of Restraint*. Minneapolis: Fortress, 2013.

Medora, John, and David White. "You Don't Own Me." *Grace Lyrics*. https://www.azlyrics.com/lyrics/grace/youdontownme.html.

"Meet the Preachers." *The Gathering, A Womanist Church*. https://www.thegatheringexperience.com/the-preachers.html.

Murray, Pauli. *Song in a Weary Throat: Memoir of an American Pilgrimage*. New York: Liveright, 2018.

Pace, Courtney. *Freedom Faith: The Womanist Vision of Prathia Hall*. Athens, GA: University of Georgia Press, 2019.

"Partner. Gather Online. Support." *The Gathering, A Womanist Church*. https://www.thegatheringexperience.com/get-connected.html.

"Pledge to End Violence Against Women." *LiveYourDream.org*. https://go.liveyourdream.org/end-violence-against-women/pledge.

Roosevelt, Franklin D. "Second Inaugural Address," January 20, 1937. *Bartleby.com*. https://www.bartleby.com/124/pres50.html.

Roy, Arundhati. "The 2004 Sydney Peace Prize Lecture." *The University of Sydney* (November 4, 2004). https://sydney.edu.au/news/84.html?newsstoryid=279.

Sampson, Melva. "Going Live: The Making of Digital Griots and Cyber Assemblies." *Practical Matters: A Journal of Religious Practices and Practical Theology* (October 16, 2019). http://practicalmattersjournal.org/2019/10/16/going-live-the-making-of-digital-griots-and-cyber-assemblies//.

Session, Irie Lynne. *Badass Women of the Bible: Inspiration from Biblical Women Who Challenged and Subverted Patriarchy*. Dallas, TX: ISIS, 2019.

———. *Murdered Souls, Resurrected Lives: Postmodern Womanist Thought in Ministry with Women Prostituted and Marginalized by Commercial Sexual Exploitation*. Charleston, SC: CreateSpace, 2015.

Shakur, Afeni. Quoted in "Key Themes Explored in Tupac Biopic 'All Eyez on Me,'" by Ashley Lyle. *Billboard* (June 15, 2017). https://www.billboard.com/articles/columns/hip-hop/7833723/tupac-biopic-all-eyez-on-me-key-themes.

Simpson, Candace. "Black Women Must Be More Than the Canaries in Your Coal Mines." *For Harriet* (December 1, 2015). http://www.forharriet.com/2015/12/black-women-can-no-longer-be-canaries.html.

Smith, Mitzi J. *I Found God in Me: A Womanist Biblical Hermeneutics Reader*. Eugene, OR: Cascade, 2015.

———. "Womanist Biblical Hermeneutics: Annotate." *YouTube* (February 8, 2017). Produced by Wipf and Stock. https://www.youtube.com/watch?v=8PiRLmKDZEI.

Turman, Eboni Marshall. *Toward a Womanist Ethic of Incarnation: Black Bodies, the Black Church, and the Council of Chalcedon*. New York: Palgrave Macmillan, 2013.

"Violence Against Women: Key Facts." *World Health Organization* (November 29, 2017). https://www.who.int/news-room/fact-sheets/detail/violence-against-women.

Walker, Alice. *The Color Purple*. New York: Houghton Mifflin Harcourt, 1982.

———. *In Search of Our Mothers' Gardens: Womanist Prose*. New York: Harcourt Brace Jovanovich, 1983.

Warrior, Robert Allen. "Canaanites, Cowboys, and Indians." *Christianity and Crisis* 49/12 (September 11, 1989) 261–65.

Waters Maxine. Quoted in "Maxine Waters Teaches the Importance of 'Reclaiming My Time,'" by Cherese Jackson. *Liberty Voice* (August 2, 2017). https://guardianlv.com/2017/08/maxine-waters-teaches-importance-reclaiming-time-video/.

Watson, Natalie K. *Introducing Feminist Ecclesiology*. Eugene, OR: Wipf & Stock, 2008.

Weems, Renita J. *Just a Sister Away: Understanding the Timeless Connection Between Women of Today and Women in the Bible*. Kindle ed. New York: Warner, 2007.

West, Cornel. Quoted in "Justice is Love Made Public." *Rewire.News* (February 14, 2013). https://rewire.news/article/2013/02/14/justice-is-love-made-public-2/.

"Who Is the Womanist? *The Gathering, A Womanist Church*. https://www.thegatheringexperience.com/who-is-the-womanist.html.

"Who We Are." *The Gathering, A Womanist Church*. https://www.thegatheringexperience.com/.

Williams, Delores. "The Salvation of Growth." *The Christian Century* 107/28 (October 10, 1990) 899.

———. *Sisters in the Wilderness: The Challenge of Womanist God-Talk*. Maryknoll, NY: Orbis, 1993.

Williams, Evan, and Laura Warner. "The Black Mambas: Saving the Rhino." *YouTube* (December 17, 2017). https://www.youtube.com/watch?v=DGmVe7noHNg.

Williams, Reggie. *Bonhoeffer's Black Jesus: Harlem Renaissance Theology and an Ethic of Resistance*. Waco, TX: Baylor University Press, 2014.

Wilson, Mark. "Were Mary and Joseph Married or Engaged at Jesus' Birth?" *Bible History Daily* (December 24, 2019). https://www.biblicalarchaeology.org/daily/biblical-topics/bible-interpretation/were-mary-and-joseph-married-or-engaged-at-jesus-birth/.

Womanist Institute. "What Manner of Woman—A Short Documentary Film." *YouTube* (November 5, 2012). https://www.youtube.com/watch?v=sUlc6L1Z9-k.

CPSIA information can be obtained
at www.ICGtesting.com
Printed in the USA
FSHW021252250121
77984FS

9 781725 274624